ROADTRIPPING

To June,

ROAD TRIPPING

ON THE MOVE WITH THE BUFFALO GALS

CONNI MASSING

BRINDLE
&GLASS

Library and Archives Canada Cataloguing in Publication
Massing, Conni L. (Conni Louise), 1958–
Roadtripping : on the move with the Buffalo Gals / Conni Massing.

ISBN 978-1-897142-47-9

1. Automobile travel—Alberta—Anecdotes. 2. Alberta—Description and travel. I. Title.

FC3667.4.M37 2010   917.12304'4   C2009-906895-8

Editor: Gillian Steward
Cover and interior design: Pete Kohut
Proofreader: Elizabeth McLachlan

Brindle & Glass is pleased to acknowledge the financial support for its publishing program from the Government of Canada through the Canada Book Fund, Canada Council for the Arts, and the province of British Columbia through the British Columbia Arts Council and the Book Publishing Tax Credit.

Mixed Sources
Cert no. SW-COC-001271
© 1996 FSC
FSC

The interior pages of this book have been printed on 100% post-consumer recycled paper, processed chlorine free, and printed with vegetable-based inks.

Brindle & Glass Publishing
www.brindleandglass.com

1 2 3 4 5 13 12 11 10

PRINTED AND BOUND IN CANADA

For my beloved Buffalo Gals.

CONTENTS

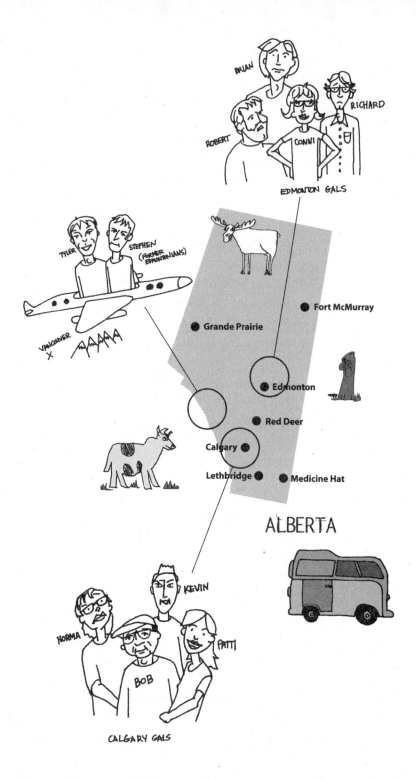

BRIAN

ROBERT

CONNI

RICHARD

EDMONTON GALS

TYLER

STEPHEN
(FORMER EDMONTONIANS)

VANCOUVER
X

Fort McMurray

Grande Prairie

Edmonton

Red Deer

Calgary

Lethbridge

Medicine Hat

ALBERTA

NORMA

KEVIN

BOB

PATTI

CALGARY GALS

PROLOGUE

There's a group of us, mostly theatre people, who have been going on a road trip together for ten years running. We call ourselves the Buffalo Gals, and every year we travel to a different region of the province of Alberta. It's such insanely good fun that I was moved to share the experience.

I grew up in a little town called Ponoka in central Alberta but have lived in Edmonton for many years. I'm a playwright and, as such, sort of the self-appointed chronicler of our adventures. However, I'd be lying if I said I wasn't worried about just a few little things . . .

The Ooga-Booga Factor
One of the best ghost stories I ever heard was about a documentary film producer trying to finish a film she'd shot of native elders sharing some secret creation myths. The images and audio just plain disappeared during a late-night editing session. Three times. The stories obviously weren't meant for public consumption.

So here's my fear. What if the YouTube video of our group scaling the giant pyrogy in Glendon, Alberta mysteriously vaporizes after this book is published? Who wants something like that on her conscience?

Will the truth actually set us free?

With that in mind, maybe I'm better off being a little flexible with the facts so as not to incite any bad karma. I've always been a firm believer that you shouldn't let the truth get in the way of a good story. I mean, really—who ever tells a story the same way twice? (And trust me, I always tell a story at least twice.) But these road trips are co-created and co-owned by several people. I guess I could have asked them all to chip in on every single memory of the nine years we've been doing this trip, but I can tell you right now that would lead to tears. Of *course* I've consulted them religiously. (Okay, we exchanged a coupla emails.) But in the end, if my pals wanna go public and say I'm a big fat liar, well then so be it. Of course I'd be a little miffed, but far better that I'm miffed than them. You see the thing is . . .

You don't want these guys mad at you. First there'd be the tongue-lashing, then the beating with raw steaks. (Then they'd cook the steaks and eat them in front of me.) Plus, between the nine of them, they could make sure I never worked in this or any other town, ever again. What if my own husband got mad at me, even though I say how handsome he is about every third paragraph?

Bottom line, just because I decided to go public about the road trips doesn't mean everyone else should be exposed. (What happens in the van stays in the van, etc.) I thought I'd totally solved this by identifying the gang as characters from Gilligan's Island instead of using their real names. Even that was nothing but trouble—I should have known everyone would want to be Ginger, the gorgeous but shallow movie starlet on the show.

The Gophers

Maybe it really boils down to one thing: dead gophers. To be more exact, a museum featuring dead, stuffed gophers. Now you either find this funny or you don't. If you do kind of, sort of, possibly think it's a concept at least worth investigating because you *might* find it amusing or strange or memorably quirky . . . then you're going straight to hell along with us. If you find this concept (the dead gopher thing) kind of appalling—and that's your perfect right—then there may be other, er, uh, elements of this book that you, uh . . .

Oh never mind. Thank you for your time. Enjoy.

"I'm a beautician, not a magician."
PHOTO: BOB ERKAMP

ONE
DEAD GOPHERS

I suppose my mother is to blame, really, for my gourmet appetite, my sentimental streak, and the genesis of the annual road trip that has become an all-consuming passion for me and my friends. The fateful moment occurred sometime during the summer of 1998; Mom casually dropped into a conversation that she planned to go on a senior's bus trip to the Torrington Gopher Hole Museum. *What?*

Torrington is a hamlet in east central Alberta. I had never been there before, though I'd visited the British counterpart close to a friend's home in north Devon. And while I have more than a passing familiarity with gophers, I'd never been to a museum starring the little fellas or any other kind of rodent.

I try to imagine what might be in a gopher museum. Displays depicting the illustrious past of gophers? Gophers and their role as collaborators during World War II? Gophers during the Inquisition? A little research yields the fact that whatever else may be going on, the gopher museum is full of dead rodents: stuffed, costumed, and displayed in dioramas. My friend in England reports the outrage amongst the animal-loving British public about the opening of this museum. Wow. Our colonial masters are offended—I must see the place for myself. Many a medieval pilgrimage has been trumped up with less justification.

News of Torrington inspires several rounds of jokes about exotic road trips amongst a group of like-minded theatre colleagues. (Not for us the first arrondissement of Paris; we'd rather go to small-town Alberta.) The dark rumours about the museum's imminent closure, due to continuing protests from animal rights activists, lend urgency to the proceedings. (Okay, probably only in my mind.) But the new year dawns and we still don't have a plan. My obsession deepens; I even include a reference to Torrington in a play I'm writing at the time.

Perhaps I felt instinctually that we could ward off the dark portents of the next millennium by fondling a stuffed gopher. (It was 1999, remember, and other folks were planning on crossing the International Date Line in a Learjet, or holing up in bomb shelters with canned beans and champagne.) Or maybe the desire to see the dead, stuffed gophers runs even deeper than that. Ahhh . . . the magnetic pull of the grotesque.

The road trip plan finally coalesces in March 1999. There's no rigorous selection process for seats in the van; we're just a casually thrown-together gaggle of pals, drawn from both Calgary and Edmonton, several of whom happen to be working together at the same theatre company that winter. While Alberta's two major cities are arch rivals in sporting matters and polar opposites in terms of political leanings, our noble little group shall rise above such petty differences.

From Edmonton, there are me, Stephen (a theatre director), his partner Tyler (a bookseller/arts administrator), and Norma, another arts administrator type. The Calgary contingent is composed of Bob (an artistic director), his partner Kevin, (a composer/musical director), John Paul (another artistic director), and Patti, yet another arts administrator.

Although our group originally hails from various areas of the country and beyond, we're all here—now—in Alberta. We're all suitably adventurous, and we're all what my Grandma Saunders would have described in glowing terms as "good eaters." What else do you need for a raucously good time?

The itinerary evolves throughout the dog days of a particularly mushy spring. Someone in the group wants to go to the Passion Play in Drumheller. Someone else has heard about a cook-your-own-steak cowboy bar out by Patricia. (All of these locales are roughly in the same south central—southeast quadrant of the province.) And of course we have our cornerstone event: the Gopher Hole Museum. The general insanity of life being what it is, no one can manage getting away for more than a weekend, and in the end it turns out we can't really get started till Saturday morning. It's a lot of itinerary to stuff into thirty-six hours but we're optimistic. (Oblivious? Ill-informed?) The flurry of planning emails reaches a hysterical pitch as the July weekend draws near. I'm excited and happy that it's actually happening, but secretly worried that we'll drive each other crazy in the van. These are *great* people—all of them—but it's a whole lot of personality to coop up in a clammy, claustrophobic little space for thirty-six hours. I'm not envisioning food fights or fisticuffs, just disturbing alterations in our delicate social structure, forever more, and . . . tense silence, simmering with subtext. (I'm a playwright=subtext is my life.)

At any rate, my eagerness to give this grand social experiment a shot overrides my horrified imaginings about imploding friendships. Baggage packed, with social anxieties tucked into the side pocket, itinerary chewed over, cooler stocked . . . we're off.

Kevin makes the ultimate sacrifice, donning the gopher head.
PHOTO: PATTI PON

TWO
THE TORRINGTON EIGHT

July 9, 1999

The Edmontonians agree to meet the Calgarians in a parking lot in front of the Capri Hotel in Red Deer, a little city roughly equidistant from Edmonton and Calgary. We're not yet referring to ourselves as the Buffalo Gals. That first year we refer to the trip, somewhat erroneously, as "The Stomp." As in "Stomp Around Alberta." ("*Stamp Around Alberta*" was a tourist travel campaign from the late seventies, capitalizing on the fame of the Calgary Stamp-ede. The Stamp Around Alberta "kit" came with a passport to be stamped at various locations. If you had enough locations stamped in your passport you could even win a simulated bronze medallion.) Vestiges of this conception of the road trip as a "stomp" turn up in planning emails for several years thereafter.

Patti has asked her friend Leonard, who lives in Red Deer, if he'll give us a tour. We're all bemused and amused by the notion of getting a tour of good old Red Deer. (I grew up about a half-hour away.)

Leonard, it turns out, takes his job very seriously. He arrives in the parking lot wearing a crisply pressed red and white striped shirt and carrying a box of Timbits. We've all been eating bread products and mainlining coffee for two hours prior to the rendezvous but that doesn't stop us from digging in.

There's something kind of bizarre about getting a tour of a place you've been to eight million times. But there's also something kind of great about seeing a place through new eyes. In case you've never had the pleasure, here are the basics:

Red Deer is a city of about eighty thousand people in the heart of Alberta's Parkland region, providing services to surrounding farming communities as well as to several large institutions. The Michener Centre, which houses mentally handicapped adults, was also the scene of the great Alberta eugenics project (sterilizing mentally handicapped and badly-behaved individuals) that finally ended in 1972, thanks to the newly-minted premier Peter Lougheed. Leonard gives us a drive-by tour of the Centre. We're a little bewildered but gracious. Then the van whirls through the grounds of Red Deer College, where I did my first year of post-secondary education. (And where I met Brian, who participated enthusiastically in the planning for year one but didn't actually manage to join us on the stomp/the roam/the hootenanny holler until 2001.)

Leonard gives us some interesting background on the architecture of Red Deer College. (The arts centre is built in the shape of a train.) We're wildly appreciative of the informational tidbits (and the Timbits) but very anxious to get to the main event, a beautiful monument to that modern-day hero: FRANCIS THE PIG.

Francis, a two hundred and forty-pound white hog, was at the abattoir being herded toward that final encounter one fine summer day in July 1990 when he decided to change the course of history.

(Remember the movie "Babe"? One of my favourite flicks EVER. And right at the beginning all the pigs are being shipped off somewhere and there are rumours about what happens once you go in the big truck, but no one's quite exactly sure what it means. Boooaahhhew!)

Francis must have had some kind of third sense about what was about to happen. There were probably a coupla shifty-eyed fellows trying to goad him onto a ramp or through a gate. And probably no one was being nice about it. (Oh, it's all very palsy-walsy when they're trying to fatten you up, but then suddenly the humans get ominously business-like.) Maybe Francis waited until the loader guys were pre-occupied, or maybe he landed a painful kick and made a run for it. Or maybe Francis was actually a *flying* pig. Hang on, sister! But the newspaper accounts of the day are only slightly less fanciful.

"After scrambling over a metre-high fence and tip-toeing through a sausage-making room, he nosed open a back door and turned his curly tail on local butcher Fred Huizing forever." (Tom Barrett, *Edmonton Journal*)

Francis escaped into the bushes surrounding the farm, and then further into the wooded area by the Red Deer River. He evaded cap-ture—and being eaten by predators—for five months! The press had a field day. (Oh, to have some good news for once.) Francis instantly became a cause celebre, referred to variously in the news as a frisky swine, a freedom-loving hog, the elusive or plucky porker, and my personal favourite, also from the *Edmonton Journal*, a "porcine Papillion."

His heroic flight from death and back bacon also inspired artists and musicians. Nancy White wrote a song called "Saving Francis's Bacon." The indie comedy troupe Three Dead Trolls in a Baggie wrote that stirring anthem—"Piggy Piggy Run Piggy Run Piggy Run," which inspired many a happy sing-a-long in our van. "Francis is the first thing in Red Deer that's caught the nation's attention for some time," said Craig Curtis, the city's director of community ser-vices. Well, no kidding.

After a few weeks of this glorious escape made good, even the most hardened pork producers wanted to give this heroic hog a break. In fact, everyone seemed to be pretty delighted about Francis' sstory except for Dick Huizing the butcher (and owner of the abat-toir Francis escaped from). Harassed by hog-lovers, including an Edmonton woman, (Antje Espinaco-Virseda, who sent Huizing two hundred bucks with the suggestion that the pig be named after Francis of Assisi), and pursued by an insurance company wanting him to pay damages on a car that collided with Francis, Huizing was soon sick of the unwelcome publicity. Regarding Francis: "I hope it's gone, I hope it left the country. I tell you, I just want it all to end."

And finally it did. Francis was captured late that fall; I like to think he *chose* to return, finally tired of raiding farm gardens and oinking at coyotes. Anyway, once he finally reappeared, he was allowed to live out the rest of his days in bucolic peace and splendour.

At least that's what it claims on the inscription at the base of the sculpture of Francis . . .

The sculpture, created by Danek Mozdzenski, is a beautiful bronze likeness of Francis, captured in a graceful leap, much as we imagine he might have cleared a fence or two in his heroic quest for freedom. There are some flowers planted around the monument. Which is on a little sort of island right smack in the middle of two very busy downtown streets. Nice. We take a *LOT* of photos. Then Leonard, our fabulous tour guide, tells us the horrible truth. Francis didn't live out his days on acres of rolling green, rubbing his pink tummy up against white picket fences or lifting his cute little snout up to the heavens to sniff for dinner.

Remember Babe singing "Jingle Bells" in the farmyard while the powers-that-be are plotting his demise?

The real story? Shortly after Francis was finally captured by pig tracker Al Marshal, he was indeed retired to an Innisfail farm, where farmer Doug Smith was given the job of taming Francis after his months in the wild. The city of Red Deer had plans to put Francis out to pasture in Waskasoo Park but presumably didn't want him gulping down kittens or ravaging curious children. Alas, Francis never got to demonstrate his people skills—he died from an infection (peritonitis) caused by one of the tranquilizer darts he was shot with when he was captured. Isn't that the most hopelessly unjust thing you've ever heard? So the inscription at the base of the sculpture is a LIE and plus—the other thing etched at the base of the beautiful bronze pig is: "Francis reminds us of the importance of hog production and processing to the economy of Red Deer."

NO, that's NOT what Francis reminds us of. Francis reminds us of freedom! And raging against the machine! Of seeing your destiny differently than others see it. He inspires balls-out courage and musical genius! Francis, WE LOVE YOU! We vow to have bacon the very next day for breakfast. That'll show 'em. That'll . . . pay tribute. Or something. But I soon discover that it's hard to get this group lined up behind an initiative . . .

Scene: A Red Deer Diner, The Gals Peruse Menus

Me: Wow, I'm still a bit shook up about Francis.

Bob: Who?

Me: Francis the pig. You know . . . the way he died and—

Tyler: Oh look—they have Canadian back bacon!

Bob: Yum—count me in. Where the hell's the waitress?

Me: Guys! I was thinking maybe I'd write a play about Francis.

Kevin: Will it be dinner theatre?

(Guffaws around the table.)

Stephen: How about breakfast theatre?

(More giggling.)

Me: Hey—come on! I was thinking maybe a children's play. A serious piece using the abattoir as a sort of allegory for . . . sort of like George Orwell's Animal Farm. You know, talking animals and—

Patti: I don't know about that but the bacon is sure talking to me!

(Applause and hoots of laughter from other unfeeling, oafish Gals.)

Norma: I'm having pork sausage!

(Stephen "high-fives" Norma—right on!)

Me: You guys are so—insensitive!

John Paul: (*mockingly*) Oh shush now—Conni wants to talk about her drama.

(A pause as I marshal my arguments.)

Kevin: (*VERY excited*) Look—you can get bacon in your omelet AND bacon on the side.

Me: Really? Wow! (*with commanding presence*) Hey, could we get some service over here?

Sigh. It's probably not too soon to emphasize that the road trip is about eating. And sometimes that means dealing with certain contradictions. Like Francis and the bacon we insist on having at our road trip diner breakfasts. Like the cute, wobbly calves admired in fields we've passed on the way to the steak restaurant. Or the frolicking lambs at the PaSu sheep farm and our five-course dinner there. (More about that later.) Mind you, we never would have visited PaSu if it weren't for the persistent lobbying of Stephen . . .

STEPHEN (PaSu-whiner, chief archivist, choral director)
Stephen is the moral epicentre of the Buffalo Gals. No, wait. Stephen's artistic vision encompasses the . . . nah. Stephen and I are probably the two people who care most about documenting the travels of the Buffalo Gals. Stephen wields a mean glue stick and is responsible for the archival map we create at the end of each trip. He always pastes the most things into the scrapbook. He even remembers things we did like, two or three years before! (Maybe it's because he goes on and on and on about things, like PaSu.) He's also wonderful at tallying our end-of-trip bills. And . . . he writes a respectable haiku. More on that later.

But back to food and the moral implications therein. I think that, as carnivores, we've done something every carnivore should be forced to do. We've looked our dinner (or breakfast) in the eye and said "we understand the sacrifice you've made so we can eat." It's not easy being at the top of the food chain.

Now we have a patch of driving ahead of us, the actual road trip part of our road trip.

We nose the van onto Highway 2 and drive like fiends toward Drumheller, about an hour and a half from Red Deer. Normally we would opt for the scenic route but we have to hurry cause we're booked for a 2 PM showing of the Canadian Badlands Passion Play. But don't take my word for it. A scan of the website reveals the following:

> Set in the heart of the Canadian Badlands, famous for its unique land formations, dinosaur burial grounds and the world famous Royal Tyrrell Museum of Paleontology . . . the Passion Play is located just south of the Red Deer River on the western outskirts of Drumheller.
>
> Be carried back 2000 years to the land and events that changed the course of history. This dramatic portrayal of the life, death and resurrection of Jesus Christ in an acoustically superb natural bowl amphitheatre will make you feel like you are actually there. The scripture-based script and music, realistic set and costumes, quality performance and remarkable similarity of the site to the Holy Land add to the experience.

We pull into the site. It's a lovely summer day but bone dry, and hot enough to tan a hide on your back porch. The impressive hoodoos loom invitingly in the distance. If it weren't for the sea of Winnebagos and minivans you could almost believe you were in the desert outside Bethlehem. Or in a café on the Left Bank. Because this is where John Paul's catering kicks in . . .

JOHN PAUL (gourmand, shit disturber, card-carrying shaman)
John Paul, affectionately known as John-Paul-George-and-Ringo, is one of those people who actually knows—and cares—about late-harvest grapes and the perfect temperature for Pinot Grigio and where you can get hand-painted tiles for your bathroom renovation. His elegant education also includes a grounding in—and a contempt for—most world religions. While we never called on his home decor skills during his time with the Gals (with

the possible exception of the van decoration initiative of the 2000 trip), we certainly benefited from his sacrilegious rants and gourmet snack provisions. Alas, his time with us was destined to be brief.

John Paul has taken it upon himself to prepare an exquisite picnic lunch for the group. We open up the back door of the van and feast on gooey brie, French baguette, Sicilian olives, and cold white wine. Thus fortified, we set off to see the drama.

To see a biblical pageant performed in the Badlands . . . really, if you've never seen a hoodoo perhaps you can't imagine what a spectacularly good idea this is. Large sand-coloured formations, shaped like giant hammertoes and clustered together, the hoodoos are staggered perfectly to provide depth of field. Continuing off to some far horizon, and topped with clear, blue sky, they provide a stunning natural backdrop for the play. We belly up to the concession for bottles of cold water, slather our tender bits with sunscreen and settle in to watch the drama unfold.

I actually don't remember a lot about the play. There is a lot of cribbing from the Bible, some quite lovely music, and if you get bored with that you can sit and marvel at how hot it must get in those authentic-looking costumes. We're much more scantily clad than the performers, and we may expire in the heat.

John Paul keeps leaning over and saying hideously irreverent things. Even without his commentary ("Ho-ly—look at the gams on Judas!"), I am starting to get restless. (I know how the story ends, after all.) I'm sitting in my sticky little chair, pouring bottled water down the front of my T-shirt in an attempt to stay cool, when I notice a white speck in the far distance. I clean my sunglasses but it's still there, and now it's on the move. I eventually realize that it's an actor in sky blue robes, leading a white donkey along a narrow trail through the hoodoos.

This is no painted backdrop. No actor pretending to see someone in the distance and asking you to imagine along with him. (Don't get me wrong, I'm happy to go along with this sort of artifice, it's one of the things I love about theatre.) But to see this real procession coming from a great distance—wow. So three-dimensional. So beautiful. Here comes hope? Or something pure and unsullied from another plane of existence . . . ? It takes blue-robe man and white donkey a very long time to make it into the foreground of the scene—I am completely riveted. In the end, it's all quite splendid.

I'm not sure the explicitly Christian message of the play is really absorbed by our ragtag band of atheists (one), lapsed Catholics (two), non-practicing Jews (two), milquetoast, waffly Protestants (three), a reformed Baptist (one), and Native American Shaman (one). (I realize the math doesn't really compute, but some of these people qualify under more than one heading.) Still, we all appreciated the spectacle. Now if only, if only there had been . . . retail opportunities. As in: souvenir T-shirts and ball caps and tea towels and postcards. Because as much as these road trips are about eating, they are also very much about shopping. At least for Patti . . .

PATTI (token visual minority, moral compass, shopping guide)
Patti is the best shopper I've ever met. Or maybe just the most active. When we're out in the wilds she spots those retail opportunities that we might otherwise miss. "Look, it's a painted rock that says 'Jesus Saves—Three Hills, Alberta.' We all better have one of those." Since Patti has an MBA, you'd think she could be more useful. Sure, she let us dress her up as Pocahontas when we tracked the historic fur-trading route in 2006. (What? Okay, got it. We won't do it again.) But how about coming up with a budget for the road trip so that we don't routinely spend about three mortgage payments travelling four hundred kilometres in a rental van for thirty-six hours?

Bottom line: no Passion Play paraphernalia for Patti or anyone else. But I now realize what a very narrow escape we had. How timing is everything in life. The play went into production in 1994, we attended in 1999, and now, checking the website, I see they've since built an interpretive centre.

The Canadian Badlands Interpretive Centre displays scale models spanning biblical history, authentic Middle East artifacts . . . visit the Passion Play costume studio and dress yourself up in Biblical Costume and have a photo taken with your friends and family.

Did you catch that last bit? I read this and I think of the horror that might have been. I've seen this crew dressed up as Clem T. GoFur (in Torrington), as crew members on the Starship Enterprise (in Vulcan), as early settlers (Fort Edmonton). These little dress-up sessions either clear the area of other tourists, alarm the locals, or frighten nearby wildlife. The thought of our merry little gang hamming it up in Joseph's Technicolour Dream Coat . . . ! Everyone fighting over the Mary Magdalene costume. Our resident shaman dissing the disciples. There could so easily have been a good old-fashioned stoning in the parking lot that day. At the very least a shunning. But since there wasn't, it was TIME FOR COLD BEER.

Wayne, Alberta is just ten miles southeast of Drumheller. On the four-mile stretch between Rosedale and Wayne you have to cross eleven one-lane bridges on a winding road through a little valley with coulees rising up on either side. Beautiful. It takes quite a lot to reduce our crabby, world-weary, snippy, irreverent group of road trippers to silent, awestruck appreciation of something larger than life inside the van. The trip through this valley pretty much accomplishes that.

The first coal mine in this area was opened in 1912. By the early thirties Wayne was home to some two thousand souls, and the thriving little town had all the regular institutions of commerce and commu-nity—a grain elevator, a lumberyard—as well as four tennis courts, a theatre, a skating rink and a dance hall. But the Depression hit hard in these parts, and by 1956 the population was down to two hundred and fifty-five. Nowadays forty hardy souls call Wayne home, and the Rosedeer Hotel is the only surviving business from the town's heyday. Heyday—hotel—we know we're on the right track.

The Rosedeer was built in 1913. The owner tells us they've renovated the honeymoon suite and now they get bookings from as far away as Europe. There's apparently even a ghost or two. One is friendly—being the pipe-puffing spirit of a previous owner, probably delighted to witness the renaissance of his hotel business. The other is the ghost of an elderly woman murdered on the third floor of the hotel, early last century.

The hotel's "Last Chance Saloon" is cute as hell and houses the only Wurlitzer Band Box in Canada. (A band box contains a small stage and seven small electronically operated band members.) So depending on your taste, it might be worth making a pilgrimage to see this. (For more on purposeful travelling see Chapter Eight, "On the Road.") Us—we don't care about no band boxes.

The bar extends out onto a patio. We head out and order a couple of pitchers of beer. The heat of the day has backed off just enough to be enjoyable instead of excruciating. A group of extremely cheerful people are clustered on the other side of the patio barbecuing hamburgers, celebrating a fortieth birthday. The hoodoos surround us. The cold beer arrives and we have our first real toast of the road trip.

It's a perfect moment. We are sun-kissed and jolly—we feel so SMART that we're here—now—drinking this beer in this company. And the fun's hardly started. It's so summer-on-the-patio perfect that we can hardly bear to think about moving on to our next destination. (We're meant to drive one hundred kilometres to Patricia for dinner.) Surely we're under no obligation to stick to our itinerary. There's food here and it smells great. Soon the sun will set . . .

Norma really wants to stay here where we have a bird in the hand. So does Stephen. Patti seems like she's leaning toward staying put as well. I'm feeling dithery, unwilling to come down on one side of the argument or the other. But then Bob weighs in; you can tell he's vaguely irritated by all this blurry prevaricating. He wants to move on to the next venue.

Such a delicate thing, this group diplomacy. Who knows what experiences you miss—or enjoy—because one person makes an impassioned plea or expresses a strong bias? And if there's a strong bias to be expressed, Bob's usually the man for the job . . .

BOB (curmudgeon, van-snoozer, bullshit detector)
Bob's always prepared to make a pronouncement on a situation. Like . . .
"I hate bed and breakfast places. I opt for the motel." Or "Turn off the

highway. Now. There better be a frickin' diner in Rimbey cause I want a hot turkey sandwich." Or . . . "This museum is stupid and their souvenirs are lame. I'll wait in the van." Please don't misunderstand—this is a good thing. I mean what if everybody on this trip was sort of mealy-mouthed and sweet and indecisive? We'd still be sitting in some Tim Horton's somewhere between Edmonton and Calgary, poring over a map and being nice.

Having over-stayed at the Rosedeer Hotel in Wayne, we take the precaution to phone ahead to Patricia. We're told the "steak pit" will be open till ten. Belted into the van, we head for . . .

THE PATRICIA HOTEL COOK-YOUR-OWN-STEAK BAR

The statisticians and politicians are always yammering about the rural–urban split. We experience it first-hand in the Patricia cook-your-own-steak bar—a cozy little joint with tons of western bric-a-brac and a sweet little corral for dancing. A big, framed poster on the wall depicts a scowly cowboy pointing out from the bucolic splendour of the scene. The inscription, in swirly, Gothic font: "Keep your city out of my country!" Alrighty, then.

We're delighted, of course. This gives us something to chew on for hours, like a big hunk of pull taffy plunked down in the middle of the table for our enjoyment. Once we've got our hook for the night or for the meal or the morning drive, everyone has a kind of context for their riffing and quipping. The big cowboy edict also gives rise to the famous "reel it in" hand signal, developed in response to the er—um—shenanigans of one of our more flamboyant members. That'd be Tyler. Actually, you can't even really say "flamboyant member" in front of someone like Tyler without unleashing a torrent of camp.

You can try this at home. Position your hands as if you're holding a fishing rod, one hand on the handle, the other on the reel. Then use your reel-holding hand to make a little backwards circle. As in—you've caught a big one and now you're going to . . . REEL IT IN. When things on the road trip are teetering on the brink of indecency, someone just makes the REEL IT IN sign and propriety is restored instantly. Usually. Occasionally. Actually it never works on Tyler.

TYLER (punster, stunt coordinator, literary advisor)
Tyler embraces every single moment of the trip. There's nothing he won't try and no photo he won't pose for. No article of clothing he won't remove for that photo. No window he won't hang out of whilst not wearing that article of clothing. We've nearly been run out of several establishments due to his er, uh . . . exuberance. Like the Patricia cook-your-own-steak bar. The flamenco dancing was particularly unwelcome at this venue. Tyler ain't no hanger-backer, I'll say that much.

Speaking of spontaneous performances in inappropriate venues . . . I think the Patricia Hotel bartender might have been initiating his get-up-a-posse phone tree before we even ordered our food.

Okay, not really. Everyone is perfectly pleasant. But we step over the line all night. Like the dog blocking the side door of the bar, close to our table—a beautiful golden retriever who lies right across the threshold, paws just centimetres inside the door, his mournful expression turned up toward the bar patrons. Every once in a while he edges into the room, stops, looks all sort of hang-dog-ish and guilty, does a doggy circle and lies down again. But all that comes later. First—we get to order . . .

Pat, our waitress, appears at the table. She's tall, sturdy, and radiates efficiency—you know she'll get the job done. But she also seems like she'd be pretty much just as happy pounding nails into a board or scraping manure off a tractor tire as dealing with people. You don't know deadpan till you've heard Pat run you through a menu. You can have beef or beef or beef on a bun. (Actually I guess they do have bison burgers, too.) We ask Pat for a recommendation.

Pat shrugs, considers, then says: "I'd have the rib-eye if I was you—chef's pressing knife to flesh even as we speak." Does that not just make your mouth water??! We jabber happily about the menu; we *are* happy, but we're also trying to ingratiate ourselves. So far that's not goin' so great. Pat could not possibly be less impressed that we've driven from Wayne to have dinner here. In fact, she obviously thinks we're a bit simple.

Soon the raw steaks arrive on paper plates, along with spuds and garlic toast (Monsieur Hangdog inches into the bar for a few seconds and lifts his nose to the air.) We take turns at the grill, dousing our steaks with condiments. The result is absolutely delicious. When the last bite is consumed, Tyler bursts into tears . . .

I can explain. We've already established that we're a bunch who enjoy our food, and sometimes the best appetizer is talking about the food before it's even been ordered. This used to be a kind of generalized rhapsodizing about the possibilities: "I am ravenous; I wonder what kind of restaurants they'll have in this town." But as the years pass, the Gals have become much more specific and er, directive: ("I want a beef dip. With coleslaw. Pull over.") Looking forward to the next meal is pretty much how we entertain ourselves in the van.

(Did I ever, at any time, insinuate that the discussions in the van were erudite, intellectual, serious, or deep? No, I did not. That way you won't be disappointed that we talk about food a lot. And the searing indictment of the war in Iraq discussed in the van during the 2003 road trip will come as a pleasant surprise.) Speaking of erudite . . .

KEVIN (musical director, choreography, quality control)
Even though Kevin's a composer and musical director by profession, he never ever leads us in song! (In fact, sometimes he sort of winces when we sing.) And I'm still waiting for the Buffalo Gals theme song to materialize. But then he does have another very important role to play. Kevin insists on higher standards for such things as wine, accommodations, and van commentary. We need some discerning taste—some vision—in this organization, let me tell ya, or we'd be camping in a leaky tent somewhere by the highway, drinking Sanka and telling knock-knock jokes.

There's only one problem with having such an incredible buildup to the food on the road trip—there's always a little letdown after the meal is done. We're all still a little bit too full to talk about the next meal. (You know, you've just eaten Christmas dinner, your mother claps her hands and says, "Mincemeat or apple pie? Both?") Van snacks being what they are, we're often not even hungry when we sit down in the restaurant. So the end of one of these meals can be downright painful.

Even if you haven't stuffed yourself to an uncomfortable degree, there's always a post-prandial lull once everyone realizes that the fun is over. For now. So there we are, in Patricia, experiencing our very first dip on the graph, on the road trip fun-oh-meter. I'd say it lasted oh, say . . . two full minutes. That's including Tyler's tears. Okay, sulking. (Did I ever say I wouldn't exaggerate?) But we have to pull ourselves together. Because we still have to drive nearly two hours to our hotel in Hanna, Alberta. (It was the only thing available in the entire area.) You should have seen Pat's face when we told her that. An eyebrow shoots up, she favours us with a little grunt. Translation: "I've seen some lunatics in my time, but you guys just about take the cake."

It's nearly 11 PM when we head for Hanna. Still jolly, though perhaps a little less boisterous in our rendition of "Run little piggy run, little piggy." When we finally pull into Hanna, we notice that there's a giant goose in front of our hotel. As we tumble sleepily out of the van we note that it will provide a great photo op the next morning . . .

After bacon, eggs, and countless cups of diner swill, we take photos in front of the giant goose. Briefly consider playing minigolf on the course set up in the interior courtyard of the hotel. (Okay, Kevin is the only one who seriously considers this.) Wander up and down Main Street which features a few lovely old buildings. All of this, especially the goose, is a bonus, since we really just came here to sleep.

Off we go—and let me tell you we are excited. Cause we are headed for Three Hills, Alberta. (No relation to the town of Two Hills in northern Alberta.) Home of the Prairie Bible Institute. Started in 1922 in an old farmhouse, the Prairie Bible Institute is the oldest bible college in the country. Why, you might ask, after the er . . . attitudinal challenges presented by the Passion Play, would this group be visiting a bible college?

Thing is, Stephen and I have a professional interest in the place, as I have adapted a novel for the stage (*The Aberhart Summer*) that has a scene or two set there. (Stephen has just directed a successful production in Calgary and we're about to reprise the experience in Edmonton.) We're thinking there must be something about the atmosphere of the place that we can absorb. We're also thinking there will be photo ops—maybe one of these could serve as an opening night card. We arrive in Three Hills, take some photos of the bible school campus and, of course, the big sign at the entrance. Two days in and we are already completely shameless about big, attention-grabbing group photos on major roadways, causing half-ton trucks to veer off the road as the gawkers gawk.

Since it has been easily two hours since we've stuffed our faces, we decide to follow up on a rumour about a Mennonite restaurant here in Three Hills. We drive toward the centre of town, feeling like intrepid explorers. Someone in the van spots a small, squat building amongst the light industrial subdivision that parallels the main drag. The sign above the building says, simply: Restaurant. Why mess around with names and such when you can just get to the point? While the big generic sign—a giant Coke billboard—suggests a certain lack of imagination, the parking lot is full of half-ton trucks. That has to be a good sign. Once inside the restaurant, we're transported . . .

Overwhelmed by the heady scent of warm butter with sugar, we wander toward the dining room in a daze. A kindly hostess in a crisp, white blouse asks if she can help us. My eyes fill with tears—she sounds so sincere. She seems like the sort of person who would actually listen. I'm just about to tell her about that time at summer camp when the other kids ganged up on me when she pats me gently on the arm and nods for the group to follow her. As we ascend to the upstairs seating area, pink-cheeked Mennonite women bustle past with orders of PIE. (Or if you don't want pie, you can order a single pyrogy that is the size of a piece of pie.)

The pies on offer are cherry, apple, raisin, banana cream, lemon meringue, and on and on and on. Baked on the premises. Full of goodness. I mean, really full of goodness, cause all these women look so radiant and chaste. Prayerful hands rolling out the pastry. Women with pure hearts adding the sugar to the berries. That's gotta taste better than anything prepared by old Sara Lee, right?

(Sorry to go on about the pie, but there's a sad resonance coming in Tour 2005, The Return Visit.)

The place is packed with farmers and church-goers who came here after the eleven o'clock service and haven't made it out of the place yet. Many of these diners are tucking into a delicious turkey dinner. It looks amazing, but even the Gals have their limits. We're just too full of breakfast—there's barely enough room for pie. We briefly consider changing our itinerary. Maybe if we walked up and down the highway between Three Hills and Trochu for three or four hours, we could work up an appetite for a meal. But once the towering slices of flapper pie arrive we are temporarily distracted . . .

And now, I don't know about anyone else, but I'm getting a funny feeling in the pit of my stomach. I'm starting to think seriously about . . . gophers. I can feel it in the rest of the group, too. What awaits us in Torrington? I also feel a looming sense of responsibility. What if it's a bust?

In the meantime, however, we still have to *get* to Torrington. And let me tell you—it is a beautiful, beautiful day for a drive. Really, you cannot imagine how beautiful. The sky is clear and endless and uniformly cornflower blue. The farmland stretches forever in all four directions. The fields of flowering canola crops could not have been more artfully gaudy if Van Gogh had been on the scene, tossing paint at the big canvas outside the van. We're careening down secondary highways, with barely another vehicle in sight. This is the heart of Alberta's parkland region: softly rolling hills, occasional stands of deciduous trees. Everywhere you look there are ripening crops— wheat, barley and that impossibly bright, buttery yellow canola. And then another field of green. Then more canola! And—and—and—

Here's the thing. Describing scenery is a bit like describing sex. You want readers to be right there with you but you don't want to embarrass them with corny images or clichés. You need to capture a unique manifestation of something that's been around forever, or in the case of scenery, since the last ice age. Maybe pornography is the answer. Just record the crude strokes, so to speak. Okay. Our trip to Torrington . . .

The sky is blue, a manly blue. The canola is yellow. Coy and beautiful. Seeming almost to throb with colour. An invitation: frolic in me. The sun is shining, so it is hot, hot, hot, baby! Field meets horizon in a wavy, sensual line. They come together and are as one. Night falls and still they are not parted.

No? But you see my problem. The other Gals aren't much help, frankly. Because that day on the road trip, that very first trip of trips, we are having a gob-smacked-by-nature moment, reduced to incoherence by the majesty of our surroundings. (And full tummies. And sleep deprivation.) It's not like we haven't seen this before. But we've never seen it in such splendid company, and in such high spirits. Still, what is it exactly about the scenery that has this effect on us?

I'll tell you what it isn't—Group of Seven. There are no craggy, taupe rock formations, no foreboding stands of pine. And here at this end of the province, there are no enormous guardian mountain peaks to frame the view. (That view on the drive on the Trans-Canada into Banff is so . . . presentational, don't you think?) This view is open-armed, challenging in its expanse.

(A friend from Ontario once told me that there was no chance anyone would mistake me for a Torontonian. I was bewildered, maybe even a little insulted. She struggled to articulate her meaning. Settled with saying my face was "so open" that I couldn't possibly be a big-city person. What else can I attribute this to but my practiced view of the horizon?)

There really isn't another vehicle for miles. Maybe the outside world has come to an end whilst we've been tracing our backcountry route between Three Hills and Torrington. Maybe that's why the Mennonite pie restaurant was so full. (What better way to experience The Rapture?) Maybe the planet has exploded into white light, except for this road and our van. Suddenly we just can't bear it for another second. We start looking for a place to pull off. But before you read this next bit . . .

Please rest assured that we have nothing but respect for farmers and their property (as you see when you get to the 2003 "Support

26

Our Beef Farmers" tour). Many of the Gals hail from good farming stock. (Actually maybe only me.) So the following was a kind of temporary insanity, a lapse in judgement, a folie, and definitely a frolic.

We pull into one of those little dirt road entrances to a field. The most perfect canola field so far. And we climb over the fence and we cavort. We lie down in the canola and stare at the sky. We caper and jig (and try really hard not to actually trample anything). We choreograph: everyone on their backs, only legs—waving foolishly—visible above the crop. We take photos of each other, including a great shot of Bob standing in the middle of a tall stand of yellow, pretending to read a new play manuscript. (He just happens to have one in his knapsack.) We joke that he could use the photo for the season brochure at his theatre company. (He does end up doing just that.) I still have a couple of these shots up on my fridge, courtesy of Norma.

NORMA (official photographer, historical animateur, museum nerd)
Norma actually enjoys museums and often knows some of the history of the area we're visiting. I think of her as our intellectual edge and fantasize that her participation lends an air of—respectability? Ha! But you know when people go on a family holiday and they have a bunch of kids in the camper and they stop at a gas station and about an hour later someone says, "Where's Betsy, anyway?" Well, that's kind of what it's like travelling with Norma. The rest of us dash through the interpretive centre and hurry back to the van to have a smoke or finish off the beef jerky. Time to go. Then we realize Norma's on a far-off ridge overlooking the highway, capturing the view with her old Pentax.

We frolic in the canola field for half an hour or so. We couldn't be happier if we were nine years old, puddle-stomping or making snow angels. We are of one mind. In fact, we could be sharing a brain right now—perhaps this is the ultimate Vulcan mind-meld. The only thing that gets us back on the road is the prospect of the Torrington Gopher Hole Museum.

Back in the van, attendance is taken. There are a few seconds silence due to sunstroke and over-stimulation. Then someone spots it. The sign.

TORRINGTON 8 KILOMETRES

The van erupts.

THREE

WEIGHING IN ON AN INTERNATIONAL CONTROVERSY

The Gopher Hole Museum and Gift Shop
Torrington Alberta

Visit the world famous
Torrington Gopher Hole Museum
And Gift shop on the corner of 2nd Avenue and 1st Street.

The museum is a whimsical portrayal of daily life
in our tranquil Village of Torrington.
There are 41 displays housing 72 mounted gophers.
Each display depicts a different theme: hockey player,
hairdresser, farmer, etc. Each character is dressed in suitable
attire to complement the artist's picturesque background.
The lighthearted scenes will take you on a magical trip
into a strange and wonderful land.

We are open from 10:00 AM to 5:00 PM
Monday through Sunday, from June 1 till September 30.
Tours are available for any size of group.
Admission: 14 years of age and over: $2.00
13 years of age and under: 50 cents
—from a handbill advertising the museum

I absolutely *love* the idea that somehow tourists are going to go out of their way to come to your tiny, isolated community simply because you have a giant bean on the outskirts of town, celebrating your community's essential history with pinto beans. Let's get the whole family in a station wagon and go look at that bean! Or goose. Or pyrogy. Oh, wait. That's exactly what the Gals are doing. Hmmmm . . .

According to an article in the *Calgary Herald* published just before we go on our trip, the group of forward-looking citizens credited with the idea for the gopher museum are now referred to as the Torrington Six. (We immediately start to refer to ourselves as the Torrington Eight.) Whilst this committee was discussing the special qualities of Torrington in an effort to discover something that might serve as a tourist attraction, one of the visionaries made an innocent jest that would change the world as we know it. Apparently it was along the lines of, "I got an idea. Let's stuff some damn gophers and charge people to look at 'em." (Torrington is definitely plagued by the little fellas.) After the laughter subsided, the committee members continued to brainstorm about the appropriate symbol to represent Torrington. And they just kept coming back to the idea of small, furry creatures . . .

"My honest opinion was that it was the silliest idea I'd ever heard," says Diane Kurta, who was chair of the Torrington tourism committee.

Still, the notion took hold and gophers prevailed. A successful application to the government was made; construction of the museum began in 1995. And man oh man, PETA (People for the Ethical Treatment of Animals) must really have an ear to the ground, because they started their campaign before the museum was even finished, sending letters of protest to the mayor, Harold Ehrman. There's a vicious rumour that the mayor responded with a postcard that said only "Get Stuffed."

Writing in the University of Calgary's newspaper "The Gauntlet" in 1999, Evan Osenton quotes PETA Wildlife Case Worker Stephanie Boyles: "We weren't trying to knock the museum . . . we felt if you were going to use stuffed animals anyway, why not use prefabricated models?" She also points out that people do not stuff real cats and place them in their windows on Halloween.

Would this be the fabled rural—urban split in action? Certainly rural folks have a different attitude toward animals. They may be respectful, but they're also eternally pragmatic. After all, an over-population of gophers does great damage to fields and thus cattle. (Cattle and horses can break their legs tripping in the gopher holes.) Badgers then follow the gopher populations and take over their burrows, enlarging them and creating even more danger for the pasturing animals. To your average prairie farmer, this cute little rodent is a full-out pest. A varmint. A nasty little critter that breeds easily and in frightening numbers.

Everybody's grandfather has a story about killing gophers and presenting their tails at the local drugstore to collect the reward. How is this different? I'll tell you. This goes beyond the practical culling of a problem population. This is a brazen parade of weirdness. A sick display of gallows humour. Also, something about turning this farmer's pest into an unapologetic sideshow that garners world attention and gooses your town's economy is sort of, well, uniquely Albertan.

The Torrington Gopher Hole Museum opened its doors on June 1, 1996—and unleashed what can only be described as a media frenzy. The Museum received many letters, some of them complimentary, some angry, others just downright heart-rending. Note the simple eloquence of this German man's plea: "Please stop killing the rats."

And so we Buffalo Gals find ourselves on the horn of an ethical dilemma. (Ouch—all eight of us on a horn, and we've just eaten pie.) Just a few kilometres short of Torrington, we pull the van over to the side of the road and write personal essays about the ethics of the museum, as a means of deciding whether or not we'll set foot in the place. Okay, everyone is too full of bacon and pie to write a proper essay. But don't you think for a second we didn't do some soul-searching.

Scene: Inside The Van, Headed For Torrington

Me: (*with measured sensitivity and intelligence*) I dunno guys. Maybe we should think this over.

Tyler: Pass the Spitz.

John Paul: Pass the wild mushroom polenta on rye crisp.

Me: I mean, did you read this article in the *Calgary Herald*? Sounds like PETA is pretty twisted out. Maybe they have a point.

Tyler: What's PETA?

Bob: Greek people use it for dipping into . . . dips.

Tyler: Heeeeheeeheeeheeee!

Me: Come on, guys! PETA stands for . . . be nice to pets!

Tyler: Be nice to dips!

John Paul: Pass de polenta!

Me: Hang on—PETA—

Patti: Princesses eat tiny amounts!

Me: No, wait—(*struggling with acronym*) P . . . E . . . E . . . T . . .

(*Kevin, irritated, looks up from his book on baroque music.*)

Kevin: Hello! P-E-T-A. People for the Ethical Treatment of Animals.

Me:	Yeah! And they're mad cause the people in Torrington—well what they did was . . .
Patti:	Killed some gophers and stuffed them?
Me:	Yeah!

(A long pause.)

Patti:	(*bewildered*) So?
Tyler:	Whoo-hoo! Are we almost there?
Me:	So, like . . . are we okay with that?
Stephen:	(*with gravitas*) Frankly, I'm more concerned about man's inhumanity to man.

(Murmurs of assent.)

Tyler:	We're out of Spitz!

(Groans.)

Patti:	Norma, what do you think? Where's Norma?!

(Shrieks and gasps of dismay.)

See? I tried to drum a little sensitivity and compassion into this crew but they were absolutely bent on seeing the poor little gophers. So . . .

Sunday, July 10, 1999
Giddy, short of sleep, full of toast and bacon, we pull into Torrington, Alberta. We know we're in the right place because the town's fire hydrants are painted as gopher heads. The streets are wide and pleasant, as if someone early last century had a grand vision for the town, or maybe they just thought they might as well have Parisian boulevards since there's no shortage of space. Now two combines could pass each other on Main Street with the greatest of ease. We park and wander, marvelling at the view stretching out beyond the edge of

town. And then we see it. The tiny unassuming building that houses the "collection." Our destination. The inspiration for the road trip. My heart sinks—how can it possibly live up to my expectations?

The facts: the Torrington Gopher Hole Museum is a smallish room containing just over forty dioramas depicting life in Torrington, using dead, stuffed gophers as the characters in each scenario. Some of the settings—the curling rink, the café, a campground—can actually be found in and around town. Other scenarios—early gopher settlers or gophers on Harleys—are slightly more fanciful. A local artist has painted the backdrops in each scenario.

I'll never forget our first few seconds in the museum. We file in, our eyes adjusting to the dim light. A couple of seconds to take it in, then the hooting and guffawing begins. I look at Bob—he's bent over at the waist, shaking with laughter. Tyler and I hug each other and squeal in each other's faces. Norma hauls out her camera. We dart erratically around the little room—shrieking at each new discovery. Come and look at this! Over here! Did you see the little bridal couple? Did you see the Olympic medal-winning gophers: fastest grain eater, fastest car dodger, and fastest hole digger?

The little rodents are meticulously costumed, the captions under each box unfailingly witty. Gopher hairdresser to client: "I'm a beautician not a magician." One gopher diner to another: "I'm feeling stuffed." My personal favourite is a scene set in the Torrington Treasury Branch: a bank robber ordering a clerk to "put yer paws up." I wonder about the subsequent meetings of the Torrington Six as they planned these details. Who wrote the captions? Who forced the gophers into their gingham dresses and tiny little suits? Who groomed the wigs? The mind reels.

You really do have to take a moment and think about these work bees. "Esther, could you help me glue some eyes onto this guy? He's our only albino gopher and I need him for this scene depicting racial tension in Jo-burg." (Committee chair Diane Kurta confirms, with a throaty chuckle, that the costuming sessions were insanely fun.)

Patti is the first to notice that there's a GIFT SHOP!

The gift shop is a little room at the back of the museum staffed by a startled-looking older woman who quails visibly when we invade her space. There are plenty of gopher-themed chachkas: calendars and postcards and teatowels, as well as local handicrafts (doilies, crocheted baby clothes) that have pretty much nothing to do with gophers. We're in retail heaven.

The clerk, who's probably a volunteer, painstakingly labours over the handwritten bills as we pile souvenirs on the counter. She calls for reinforcements. Minutes later, another woman arrives and rolls up her sleeves. We spend, spend, spend. We squawk, we squeal, we hoot and holler. We're to be forgiven, I hope. We love the museum—we just want something to remind ourselves of the experience. (Like we'll ever, ever forget.) We drop about three hundred dollars in twenty minutes.

By now, our biggest achievement on this road trip may be that we've left behind a trail of no-nonsense small-town Alberta women, shaking their heads about the flaky city folks who just blew through town and seemed inordinately—absurdly—excited by a) steak, b) pie, or c) gophers. I mean, it's perfectly fine that you partook of the steak and pie and dead gophers, but surely you can enjoy yourselves without making such a fuss.

Case in point: We finally leave the museum but discover that there's an enormous Clem T. Gofur head outside to be donned for a photo op or two or three. Kevin indulges us by pulling on the gopher head and cavorting in a gopher-like fashion. We try not to think about all the other people who have donned Clem T., and the bits of spit and mucus that are surely imbedded in the plaster. (What a good sport you are, Kevin!) Eventually we go and get the gift shop clerk to take the group photo. She obliges, but I think she'll be darn glad when we get out of town so she can go back to reading her romance novel.

And there's more: an enormous Clem T. Gofur monument on the edge of town. Several decorated yards around town. A little general store where we buy pop and water and generally stock up for the final leg of our journey.

A last little note about the Torrington Gopher Hole Museum. A small red flag of warning, really. It's entirely possible that you'll drive all the way there, have a look around, and not find it funny. You may not be in the least offended, but you may not find it amusing either. A family friend went for a visit after hearing me go on and on about it. Soon afterwards she cornered me at a social gathering: "We went to the Gopher Museum. I didn't find it that funny." Then she just looked at me. Like . . . explain the joke. If you've ever tried explaining your sense of humour to someone, you know how futile this was destined to be. So, there you go—you've been warned.

About 4 PM we finally leave Torrington and head for a strip of eateries and service stations on the highway just outside Red Deer, appealingly named "Gasoline Alley." We pull into Glen's Teacup Restaurant to have a last meal together before we part ways. And guess what? The daily special is roast turkey with all the fixins'—all our culinary dreams have come true.

We also have to do our accounts. We've spent hundreds of dollars, eaten about ten thousand calories—each—and logged a spectacular twelve hundred kilometres in approximately thirty-six hours. We're out of our minds with exhaustion. But somewhere along the way— maybe it was around the table at the Wayne bar, or over breakfast in Hanna—we started talking about next year's road trip. And as we all know, after you successfully complete a road trip, and even once discuss the possibility of repeating the experience, you have created a TRADITION!

The Rapture in the Canola.
PHOTO: PATTI PON

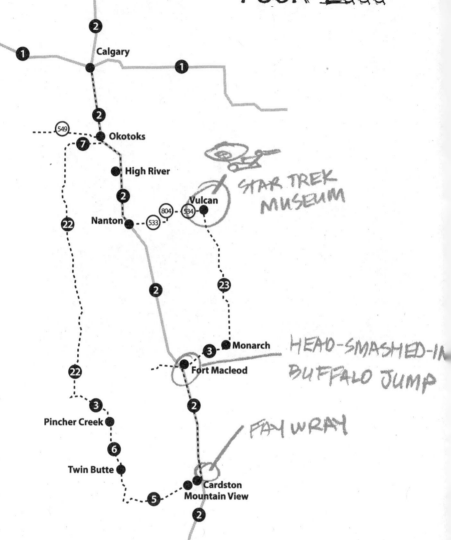

TOUR 2000

STAR TREK
MUSEUM

HEAD-SMASHED-IN
BUFFALO JUMP

FAY WRAY

FOUR

THE PREAMBLE

Subject: I LOVE it when a plan starts comin' together
Date: 7/12/2000 4:34:28 PM Mountain Daylight Time
From: Patti
To: The gals

Okay kiddies,

With only 10 SLEEPS LEFT we got some options that I wanna put on the table for us to munch on.

The following is a tentative itinerary:

Saturday

9:00 AM depart for Millarville market for breakfast and food provisions for the weekend.

11:30 AM head to Longview (Optional stop at Bar U Ranch—it's the one that the Prince of Wales owned).

2:30–6:00 PM head down the Crowsnest Pass to Frank Slide or Bellevue mines, then swing back over to "Pincher Creek?!?!?" area where we can see the Crystal Village and have our picture taken beside the road sign.

6:00 PM find the lovely Payne Lake Lodge that I have rented for the night overlooking Payne Lake and the Mountains (the cost was 300 +taxes so divided up by 9 it comes to $38 each which was roughly what we were gonna have to pay for a motel). There are 6 bedrooms, a full kitchen and living/dining room which we have to ourselves. The proprietors live in a separate suite downstairs.

7:00 PM head to the Great Canadian Barn Dance for the BBQ beef dinner and some old tyme music and dancing!

10:00 PM head back to the lodge for a lovely nightcap and some fellowship.

Sunday

?AM we cook breakfast and have a lovely morning visit.

10:30 AM head to Cardston for some Mormon fun and frolicking.

12:30 PM off to Head-Smashed-In for some pow-wow adventures and retail therapy.

3:30 PM leave for High River to have a lookie at the murals and a lovely steak dinner at the place John Paul recommends.

6:00 PM take Tyler and Stephen to the aeropuerto and begin planning for next year's adventure up north!

Now of course ALL of this is subject to change to whatever people want to do. What I wanted to ask in particular was if everyone was okay with the overnight accommodation. In addition to booking the lodge, I also made some reservations at the Flamingo Motel in Cardston, and it is roughly the same price. Don't know for certain if Cardston is a dry town or not, but at least at Payne Lodge it doesn't matter. As for Saturday night festivities there are also theatre options at the Cardston Summer Theatre (Encore—a musical revue of music from the 1920s through to the 1990s!) and "Haunting Melody" at the Empress Theatre in Fort Macleod. Oh the possibilities are endless!

So that's what I have to share with the class so far. I know that Stephen, Tyler, Conni and Robert arrive in Calgary Friday. Norma is looking to see if her schedule will allow her to come Friday night too, cuz it would be more fun if we could all congregate in Calgary rather than make her drive out to Millarville.

Okay kids, that's the update for now.

Hugs!

Patti

The above is a taste of the Buffalo Gals process, distinguished by two things:

1. The emails are intended to facilitate planning and of course that's going to involve a certain amount of anticipation. But this healthy and normal activity has grown into such feverish and frantic fantasizing that we somehow manage to mythologize the trip before we've even begun. Surely this is just courting disaster. How can any trip live up to these towering expectations? So far we've never really been truly disappointed but—mark my words—this can't end well.

2. Projections about activities to be completed (or even begun) before noon are completely unrealistic due to our absolute inability to get on the road in any kind of timely fashion. The morning schedule proposed in the above is completely laughable. (I know this now, though it sounded good at the time.) After years of going on this road trip, I continue to be puzzled by this phenomenon. It's a kind of inexplicable domestic voodoo magic, like socks disappearing or the Virgin Mary appearing on the side of a half-ton truck.

You see the thing is, this is a group who eats on time, lemme tell you, unless there's some kind of natural disaster (extensive flooding during Tour 2005) or inexplicable Sunday closings of small town cafés (Tour 2004). My point is, in the morning we always roll out of bed and go directly to the appointed dining establishment. Always. And it's always a sort of snappy, expeditious affair. (Like bacon and eggs, coffee on an IV drip, boom, you're done.) So then what the hell happens?

Perhaps this annotated version of Patti's email will give you some idea of how things actually play out at the beginning of one of our trips . . .

Subject: I LOVE it when a plan starts comin' together
Date: 7/12/2000 4:34:28 PM Mountain Daylight Time
From: Patti
To: The gals

Okay kiddies,

With only 10 SLEEPS LEFT we got some options that I wanna put on the table for us to munch on.

The following is a tentative itinerary: (I'M ALREADY HOLDING MY SIDES—OH, THE HILARITY OF THAT WORD: ITINERARY!)

Saturday:

9:00 AM depart for Millarville market for breakfast and food provisions for the weekend.

OKAY, NOT SO MUCH. WE EDMONTONIANS SLEEP OVERNIGHT AT PATTI'S HOUSE. WE GET UP, HAVE COFFEE, PHONE THE OTHER CALGARY GALS TO MAKE A PLAN ABOUT MEETING. HAVE SOME MORE COFFEE. PLAY WITH PATTI'S DOG. GO TO MEET STEPHEN AND TYLER AT A NEARBY BREAKFAST PLACE. WE'RE HARDLY ON THE ROAD THREE MINUTES WHEN WE HAVE TO TURN AROUND AND GO BACK TO PATTI'S. (I LEFT MY COSMETICS BAG HANGING ON THE BACK OF HER BATHROOM DOOR.) OKAY WE'RE OFF. AGAIN. WE MEET STEPHEN AND TYLER AT "PRIMAL GROUNDS." WE DRINK COFFEE—WE EAT PASTRY—WE READ THE PAPER. THEN WE DO IT ALL OVER AGAIN, ONLY THIS TIME WE READ THE CLASSIFIED ADS. FINALLY THE VAN PULLS UP WITH THE OTHER CALGARIANS. TYLER HAS TO PEE. OH WAIT, EVERYONE HAS TO PEE. OH NOW WE'RE ON THE ROAD. OH NO WE'RE NOT. EVERYONE WHO'S ELIGIBLE TO DRIVE HAS TO LEAVE A PHOTOCOPY OF THEIR LICENSE WITH THE RENTAL AGENCY.

AT 12:10 PM WE LEAVE CALGARY CITY LIMITS.

So there you go—we're finally on the road and it's practically time for lunch. Rest assured about one thing. The next year, around this time, we will be trotting out exactly the same totally unrealistic itinerary. Some things never change. However . . .

The world turned and turned between Buffalo Gals 1999 and 2000. Stephen accepted a job teaching at the University of British Columbia in Vancouver. So now he and Tyler have to fly in for the Gals' weekend. One more real life note: by July 2000, I was about to move in with my future husband, Bob. (Heretofore known as Robert so as not to be confused with Bob.) So it seemed logical to bring him along on the road trip . . .

ROBERT (transportation captain, webmaster, research coordinator)
Robert is a bona fide introvert thrown into the shark-infested waters of van talk. (e.g.,"Whubba, whubba, wha-hoo, there's the sign for Drumheller, didya see the sign? Whahoo, pass the chips, will ya? What's that smell? Haaaaa . . .") And so on. When Robert does participate in the badinage, he chooses his opportunities wisely, rarely weighing in about operatic tenors (doesn't know, doesn't care), but occasionally serving up wry witticisms—and bad puns—relating to other important issues such as roadkill and map-reading. Anyhow, personally I just think he's so terribly, terribly brave for coming on this trip with all these theatre folks. (He's a computer geek.) Think of the endless conversations about set design or directorial concept to be endured. Then there's the moral decrepitude (creeping soul rot), so endemic to this profession. What if he should be corrupted?

Of course everyone knows how unnerving it can be to introduce a new boyfriend to a group of old friends. By July 2000, I am a nervous wreck. I'm not inviting this guy to coffee for twenty minutes of polite conversation and a surreptitious "vetting." We are going to spend two days together!!

One more thing of note. This trip may well have seen the start of the infamous PaSu-whining that eventually led to us indulging the desires of our dear Stephen. For years, every single time we drove down Highway 2 and saw the sign for PaSu sheep farm (about forty-five minutes northwest of Calgary, near Carstairs), there would be such a din of plaintive baaa-ing and mewling—I can't tell you what we've endured over the years. We Gals are nothing if not long-suffering . . .

The Gals Land in Vulcan.

FIVE

WHERE THE BEEF IS . . .

PRESENT:

Patti, Norma, Robert, Conni, Stephen, Tyler, Bob, John Paul

ABSENT:

Kevin

When we eventually get past Calgary city limits we head for the Millarville farmer's market, one of the best examples in the entire province of this glorious tradition.

A mere thirty minutes or so to the southwest of Cowtown, this food and craft fair is a favourite Saturday outing for Calgarians.

We Buffalo Gals certainly appreciate any opportunity to spend money and there's plenty of options here in Millarville. We buy splendid provisions for our Sunday breakfast as well as van snacks, handicrafts, and some fairy wings and a sceptre for Patti. (The latter is in appreciation of her deft and tireless trip organization.)

We're also inspired to decorate the van this time out. Tyler is deemed the arbiter of taste on this matter—possibly a mistake—and though he does a bang-up job with the supplies at hand (toilet paper)— it's the first time on the trip that we fantasize about having a proper craft bag. (For a list of THINGS YOU SHOULD TAKE ON YOUR ROAD TRIP, including a craft bag, please refer to Appendix One.)

Soon after Millarville we continue with one of the Buffalo Gals' most storied traditions. A ritual that has such depth of feeling attached to it that mere words don't seem adequate to describe it. A rite of passage for aspiring Gals everywhere, and nothing less than the crucible of our experience on this trip.

Tucking into the beef.

As we herd the van down Highway 22 toward cowboy country, we lick our chops at the prospect of Longview's most famous export (besides Ian Tyson): beef jerky. We stop at the tiny store that sits right on the highway across from the fire station. They have several different kinds of jerky (teriyaki, barbecue, regular, etc.) and we try them all.

We stand around the front of the store and eat some there. We load up the van with jerky. We stare up and down the beautiful valley at the "long view" this town is named for, whilst munching more jerky. We're in cowboy country and it's dead pretty. There's still a few real working ranches out here—Ian Tyson's doing his best to stop this area of the country from being eaten up by developers and oil companies. (If we'd made time in the itinerary we could have visited the famous Bar U Ranch, operational till 1950, and now a National Historic Site.) Anyhow, if you're out in this neck of the woods, gaze out at the foothills, cast your mind back fifty years, and let this stanza run through your head, courtesy of cowgirl poet Doris Daley.

> We knew drought and fire and heartache
> We knew fat and we knew bone
> But we were silver lining people and we never rode alone

Silver lining people, huh? Nice.

Now I feel like we've finally started the trip. We've had breakfast, we finished all the necessary paperwork, we actually made it out of

46

Calgary, we have bought provisions, decorated the van—and Patti—and now we have snacks. Let the games begin!

After Longview we decide to be spontaneous. Next time we decide to be spontaneous I hope someone knocks us upside the head. But here's the thing: we see a sign for a Magnetic Hill, between Nanton and Highway 22. A magnetic hill is a place where the surrounding topography creates the optical illusion that a very slight downhill slope appears to be an uphill slope. Ergo, a car left out of gear will appear to be rolling uphill.

Probably the most famous Canadian version of this magical phenomenon is found in New Brunswick. I imagine long lineups of cars and RVs, "Magnetic Hill" hotels and restaurants. Kiosks selling "Magnetic Hill" souvenirs. Who knew we had one of these things in Alberta?

We make the detour onto a gravel road. It's pretty unprepossessing so far. Oh wait, here's a hill. And a sign. We follow the instructions. Wait to be sucked into another dimension. Take turns standing out on the road to observe the magic. Nothing. I guess all that jerky and the retail purchases from the Millarville market have loaded us down—we're beyond the forces of magnetic magic. We make more people get out of the van for the next try but to no avail. Heck, we can barely get the van up the hill with the engine going and the pedal to the floor, never mind with our will and imagination. And that's all right, because I see this as the emotional preparation for a sad fact of road trip life:

Sometimes things are just kind of lame.

Now that we've been at this awhile we have a long list of lame-oh attractions to our credit. Who can forget the Perryvale General Store? The Vilna Mushroom? The Castor Beaver? All in good time. But this was the beginning, the first test of our character. Would we throw tantrums? Complain to management? Kick the tires of the van? Well, yes. But in the end we just give up and get back onto Highway 22.

Highway 22 is just flat-out one of the most gorgeous highways you will travel anywhere on earth. It runs down the west side of the province from northwest of Edmonton (around Mayerthorpe) to just east of the Crowsnest Pass. Every single minute, there's something spectacular to look at on the west side of the road. From about Rocky Mountain House onward you're looking at, well, Rocky Mountains. Where we are now, around Longview, the horizon softens into big, rounded foothills off to the west. Years later, a truck barrelling down this highway at twilight will be the opening shot of Ang Lee's film, *Brokeback Mountain*.

I must confess something. When it comes to scenery, this is my favourite area of the province . . .

It's now four o'clock and we're still a long way from our accommodations and our evening's entertainment in Mountain View. We've already figured out that there won't be time to do the Crowsnest Pass, but we may not even have the time to go to the Crystal Village. Crystal Village: thirteen buildings handmade out of two hundred thousand glass telephone insulators and nine hundred telephone line crossarms.

I'm sorry we've missed this—it sounds like it would be right up our alley. Would it be cheesy? I imagine so. Is cheesy what we're after? Absolutely. But it's more complicated than that. We admire and appreciate the kind of quirky ingenuity that inspires these mad concoctions. What possesses people?

Of course I have a theory. I believe these things are the result of thwarted or suppressed creativity. I'm sure there's a farmer out there who puts in long hours on the combine dreaming about painting the ceiling of the Sistine Chapel. Or designing an opera house. Maybe he just doesn't feel like he can afford to go off and study architecture just now. He's gotta get the crop off, he's gotta feed six kids, and really, he's pretty happy being a farmer. But something eats at him, just a little, as he contemplates all that space. And that creativity will out itself eventually, sometime and somehow.

Given limited raw materials, the artist's vision sometimes warps into something quite um, er . . . quirky. Like the entire village of people made from hay bales and old tires, set up in the front yard of a farmer on a desolate stretch of road near Two Hills. (Tour 2001.) Or the ball of cigarette paper in the Lac La Biche Museum. (I'll explain later.) Or stuffed gophers. Or . . . this Crystal Village thing.

We do make time, however, to pose for a photo in front of the sign for the town of Pincher Creek. Mostly for the sake of a very silly and endlessly diverting little joke. A little bonbon of wordplay that amuses us no end in the van. (Cut us some slack, we spend many, many hours there. One really does tire of dissecting Proust or playing spot-the-trope.)

It's a very old joke that experienced a renaissance when the Alberta government privatized all the liquor stores in the province. Stores formerly run by the Alberta Liquor Control Board became "Liquor Depot" or "Liquor Barn." If you emphasize the first syllable of both words and say "Liq-uor De-pot!" with a lascivious (and enthusiastic) lift to your voice . . . see what I mean? And if you like you can add insult to injury by following up with . . . "But I hardly know her!"

Okay, okay—I've just explained a joke. But knowing that we're amused by this actually explains a lot about our little gang. As in, perhaps you can see why we really did have to take a group picture around the big sign that says: "Pinch—er Creek". (I direct you to Appendix Three "Weed whackers" for variations on this theme.)

We continue down Highway 5 south, another astonishing piece of road, just skirting the edge of Waterton Lakes National Park. We stop for a couple of photos. I have the most spectacular shot of Patti and I nestled up together on a large, flat rock, with the world dropping away behind us. It is getting nigh on to cocktail hour when the Buffalo Gals van pulls into the yard of Payne Lake Lodge.

Imagine. The handsome "intended" goes to the beautiful but iso-lated Pain-I-mean-Payne Mountain Lodge, to spend a night with the nearest and dearest of the beautiful young heroine. (Yeah, yeah—it's called literary license.)

The "lodge" is actually a monstrously large house—think suburban mansion and then double it. There's a lake in front of the lodge—as promised—and then nothing else as far as the eye can see. It's beautiful, sure, but awfully darn quiet. The Gals pile out of the van and stam-pede toward the lodge. We knock at the door. No response. Stephen tentatively pulls open the screen door, which screeches like a scalded cat. Hello? Nothing. He walks in, and we tumble in behind. We slip off our shoes and make our way down a hallway that opens out into a spacious great room, with large windows featuring a stunning view of Payne Lake . . .

. . . which would turn out to be so aptly named . . .

PERIL AT PAIN LAKE—a Prairie Gothic

"Welcome to Payne Lake Lodge." The voice is melodious and yet menacing.

We're startled half out of our wits as we wheel around to see our hostess. She is an attractive middle-aged woman who says her name is Linda. I can hardly credit this introduction. She looks far more like a Deirdre or a Livinia. And as for the welcome . . . when she casts a glance over our group there's a maniacal glint in what I do believe is a glass eye.

We wonder why anyone would build a country house this big. Livinia tells us that she and her husband are only the caretakers—the property is owned by a Japanese woman who built the lodge because she'd planned to open a school for Japanese girls to learn English. Then somehow this plan failed to materialize and the owner went back to Osaka. Why, we ask? Livinia's evasive. She murmurs something about the yen falling.

(Or perhaps there was some kind of hideous accident. Perhaps they had the inaugural session with a small group of acolytes and one of them died mysteriously and perhaps the police never investigated because they were never quite clear on how many girls were here in the first place. And late at night, if you listen, you can hear crying . . . down on the shores of Pain Lake.)

Actually we might have a got a more satisfying explanation out of Livinia, only just then John Paul nudges me and whispers, "Look up!"

Peering down at us are several massive stuffed mountain sheep heads arranged in a ghastly gallery around the upper level. Livinia mistakes our horrified fascination for admiration.

"My husband's one of the few hunters in the world to bag the Big Six," she says proudly.

Now that we really look around us we see grisly trophies everywhere. There are birds of prey and small woodland creatures standing on their hind legs—forever. A fierce-looking eagle mounted on the wall beside what will be my bedroom looks poised to take a dizzying dive toward some unsuspecting prey. It looks as though it could peck out my eyes while I sleep. I must confess to a rare surge of hysteria just at that moment. Luckily Sweet Robert is there to hold my arm and stroke my brow. The palpitations soon pass.

Was this nature's revenge on us for laughing so heartily at the stuffed gophers? Long-dead mountain sheep with mournful eyes overseeing our revelries? Malevolent birds swooping o'er our heads? Were we doomed to experience the taxidermy tour year after year? To be tormented by the cruel morbidity of stuffing forevermore?!

I am getting breathless again; Sweet Robert helps me loosen my collar. I'm not sure, but he may have also copped a feel.

Thank heavens Kevin lugs in the cooler whilst the ladies are touring the bedrooms. He's already started on the refreshments by the time we regain the main floor. A gin and tonic is sure to restore our equilibrium!

Tyler offers said beverage to Livinia. She politely declines and excuses herself, descending to the basement. How curious, I observe, little thinking of the ill portended by Livinia's over-hasty exit. It is then we notice that not only is the lodge bedecked with wildlife, but there are several photos of Mormon temples featured in the décor. No doubt we had offended our host's religious sensibilities with the offer of gin. We vow not to repeat the error.

Stephen catches a glimpse of a strange figure outside in the yard. Could it be Livinia's husband Boris, the great hunter?

We've just settled in with our second round of cocktails when Livinia returns. She quizzes the group about our plans for the evening. The conversation stalls awkwardly at least three times but still she hovers. Finally a loud thumping is heard from the lower levels of the lodge. Livinia's eyes widen and she excuses herself. Oh the horror, the horror . . .

Soon it's time to leave for the Great Canadian Barn Dance, about half an hour's drive north of the Lodge.

We arrive in time for a tasty barbecue dinner—beef with all the fixins and plenty of soft drinks. There's lively country–bluegrass music and though I think it's highly unlikely that we'll dance, it may be enjoyable to watch others fling themselves about. The "barn" over-looks a pretty little man-made lake, where one can borrow brightly coloured paddleboats for sweetly unadventurous trips across the pond. (We do.) We also take a long, pleasantly meandering hayride around the lake.

The whole event is charming beyond belief. Almost too charming. I, for one, feel quite old and jaded in comparison to this crowd enjoy-ing themselves thoroughly without the benefit of a nice Australian Shiraz or a couple of purloined cigarettes. Wholesome food, music, and family activities. Wholesome, wholesome, wholesome—I nearly slip into a coma. If there'd been an opium den down the road, we'd have gone directly there afterwards for a little antidote to all the innocent fun. Knowing there was no such prospect, I'm in grave danger of standing on a picnic table and yelling obscenities, just to break the spell. It's time to leave.

We start to gather ourselves. Norma has to be retrieved from the far end of the hayride loop, as she's busy snapping photos of combines or cows or something. (Norma really does take the most glorious photos of our adventures and I suppose we should be grateful for that. I certainly am, since my own collection features many a blurry shot of red-eyed Buffalo Gals showing their back teeth as they guffaw unattractively under unflattering light, composition all askew.)

It's after ten o'clock and still light enough that you could read a newspaper standing in the parking lot amongst the half-ton trucks. But as we wait for Norma to join us, clouds gather . . .

We hurtle down a country road as the sky darkens from summer evening blue to slate grey in moments. A boiling front of ugly weather is chasing us down the highway. We drive at a brisk pace with hope of beating the storm but are soon overtaken. Might as well enjoy it . . .

Stirring instrumental music ("Hold On" from Outback's CD *Baka*) plays on the van stereo. After the first crack of thunder, the driver cranks up the volume. Loud. (We ain't talkin' anyway—we're having a gobsmacked-by-nature moment.) Sheets of lightning flash across the horizon. We hold our breath waiting for the thunderous clap to follow. The storm surges and subsides and then makes a roaring comeback. Kabooms and flashes in every direction. It's a relief when the heavens finally open and it starts to pour.

The rain has transformed the Lodge's narrow driveway into a treacherous, muddy trough, but Sweet Robert is equal to the task, delivering us safely to the door. We hurry inside, soaked through. (I, for one, am wishing there'd been room for my lady's maid in the van.)

We enter the dark hall of Payne Lodge. There has evidently been a power outage in our absence. We're in complete darkness save for the light of the storm seen through the front windows of the lodge (and reflected in the gleaming eyes of the dead animals). Livinia's nowhere to be found, but there are candles set out for our use. We are still of good cheer, placing pretty, flickering lights on tables and preparing refreshments.

John Paul is the first to spot the alteration that has taken place in our absence—all of the Mormon icons have been removed from the premises. The painting of the Cardston Temple on top of the piano— gone. The Christ-on-the-Cross wall hanging—poof.

Stephen takes the quite reasonable view that Livinia has removed them to make us more comfortable. I confess to a sense of creeping dread. Perhaps the photos and icons and paintings have been removed so they'll not be witness to . . . events. "What events?" demands Stephen, somewhat querulous. I shake my head, ashamed of having expressed a dark fancy. Just then, a crash of thunder. And right on its heels, as if knowing the stage has been set . . .

A dark shape swoops overhead! Patti and Norma scream in unison. I clutch at Sweet Robert's arm. Is it a bat? Or perhaps some dark phantasm meant to augur our doom? It swoops again, lower this time. Patti faints. As does Norma—and Tyler.

John Paul observes darkly—with astonishing prescience, it turns out—that we're falling like flies and not a shot has been fired. Then he, too, faints dead away. I am made of somewhat sterner stuff but do feel a bit light-headed at the sight of our friends piled up in a ghastly heap. Stephen quite sensibly runs to get water and damp cloths to restore the fallen. Kevin plays a frantic tarantella on the grand piano. Bob complains bitterly that the ice meant for his gin and tonic has melted.

Another flash of lightning illuminates the front window, and those of us left standing see the silhouette of a man standing on the terrace overlooking the lake. Could it be the mysterious Boris? Is that a rifle he's holding, or is he just happy to see us? Kevin, Stephen, and Bob all succumb to the shock, slumping to the floor.

A clap of thunder and Boris turns to face us. He smiles malevolently. Mouths the words: "I wanna bag me the big eight." Sweet Robert bursts out onto the balcony and charges Boris. And that's the last thing I remember . . .

I'm awakened gently by a cold compress. Sweet Robert has saved us all, by driving Boris off the balcony into the lake and to his death. Or no . . . it may be the whole incident was a horrid fancy, a product of our over-active imaginations, or, as Scrooge speculates in *A Christmas Carol*, a "bit of undigested beef." Still, Sweet Robert is our hero! And that night, we are not parted . . .

We make ourselves a splendid breakfast with the supplies from the Millarville farmer's market: eggs, toast made from freshly-baked bread, spread with homemade raspberry preserves. And coffee. Lots and lots of coffee. After an exceedingly pleasant interlude of sitting on the outside deck, or walking along the shore of Payne Lake, we reluctantly load up the van.

The little town of Cardston, home to about four thousand souls, was settled in 1887 and named after Charles Ord Card, the son-in-law of Brigham Young. The hardy pioneers who joined Card in this early settlement barely got a roof over their own heads before they started building the temple.

A sprawling edifice of pale-coloured granite, the temple opened in 1923 after ten years of construction. It's impressive, to be sure—truly awe-inspiring. But then you know this group and organized religion.

Some of the Gals do the tour of the premises (through the sections where we're permitted) and the others lounge on the lawn. There's another religious experience awaiting us just blocks away. Remember that song from *Rocky Horror Picture Show* that Frankenfurter sings during the floor show?

"What ever happened to . . . Fay Wray?"

Born in Cardston in 1907, Fay Wray played the ultimate damsel in distress in the 1933 version of *King Kong*, and will forever be associated with the role. There's a lovely tribute to her in downtown Cardston, a wrought iron cut-out of her and King Kong, right beside a little stone fountain. For reasons that really do escape me now, we all decided that we should take little vials of Fay Wray water as souvenirs. Some sort of Fountain of Youth thing, no doubt. Everyone seems much happier having paid tribute at the altar of Hollywood stardom rather than at the Mormon temple.

Swooning over the Big Boy in Cardston.
PHOTO: NORMA LOCK

On the road again, we're finally pointed more or less north on Highway 2. The last leg of our journey will take us to Head-Smashed-In Buffalo Jump and points beyond. The mood in the van: we're completely exhausted. Full of toast and coffee. (Although when someone finds a bag of jerky wedged between two seats, we make short work.) Some of us have been to Head-Smashed-In before and are sporting fabulous T-shirts from their gift shop. This place has the best logo ever. Imagine a line of gold-stitched buffalo making their way across your chest. Then suddenly, just to the other side of your left breast, the last buffalo takes a dive off the cliff. Some of the more shallow members of our crew are pretty darn excited about the retail opportunities sure to be available in the gift shop. Some of those same shallow Gals have moved on from their pathetic "Pin-cher Creek" humour to jokes about how they must answer the phone at the interpretive centre here. "Good morning, Head-Smashed-In" or "Head-Smashed-In—how may I help you?" I never said we were classy.

Located eighteen kilometres north and west of Fort Macleod, at the juncture between the foothills of the Rocky Mountains and the great plains, Head-Smashed-In is one of the world's oldest, largest, and best-preserved buffalo jumps. It was used for fifty-five hundred years by Plains Aboriginal peoples to kill buffalo by driving them off a ten metre high cliff. The buffalo carcasses were then processed at a nearby camp. According to legend a young Blackfoot wanted to see the buffalo plunge off the cliff but ended up getting buried under the pile of carcasses. He was found later with, you guessed it—his head smashed in.

(Some of the accounts refer to the animals in question as bison whereas some call them buffalo. I think we're going to go with buffalo, since I can't imagine us calling ourselves the "Bison Gals." Let's try singing it just to complete the experiment. "Bison Gal, won't you come out tonight, come out tonight . . ." You see what I mean.)

Head-Smashed-In Buffalo Jump is a World Heritage Site, and with good reason. It's not about an edifice—like a pyramid or a Taj Mahal—and not exactly the same as the Great Barrier Reef or the Grand Canyon, natural marvels created without the intervention of man. It's more about a feeling . . .

It's certainly striking to see, too—don't get me wrong. And the approach to it is both bewildering and thrilling. You herd the van onto tiny Highway 785. You wind your way through some mighty spacious countryside, past little ranches and farms. Around each bend you think, surely now there'll be a big sign and we'll see the interpretive centre. Absolutely nothing in sight. You check the map—you're on the right road. You peer up at that huge wedge of land that must be the jump. Nothing.

Suddenly you're there. The interpretive centre has been built right into the hill; it's the colour of gravel, blending in perfectly with the pale grasses and dirt. The building is beautifully designed; the contents are intelligently laid out and terribly informative. You shouldn't miss it. But after that you should go outside and walk and walk and walk on one of the trails provided. These paths meander to various vantage points. You can also stumble across ongoing archeological digs. I say, pick a bench, sit down, and listen.

Now that you're up here you can see a very, very long way in every direction. The air is hazy, softening the outline of large topographical features, like Chief Mountain, to the south. You close your eyes. The sun warms your face and the grasses whisper. You feel transported somewhere else and absolutely rooted to this spot, all at once. There's a strong spirit here: a feeling of "always was, ever will be."

We feel particularly lucky on the day we visit Head-Smashed-In as there's a powwow taking place just below the interpretive centre. We wander the site, watch the fancy dancers strut their stuff, admire the costumes, eye the merchandise in the craft tents.

Between the whispering wind and the Native drumming we're all in a sort of trance. It takes ages to round up the group this time. But we have to leave—we've got at least two hours travel time ahead, a meal to consume, and . . .

. . . an absolutely compulsory visit to Vulcan, Alberta, population two thousand. (Sorta halfway between Lethbridge and Calgary.) There's obviously been a different sort of energy here right from the very beginning—Vulcan's founder named the town after the Roman

God of fire. Originally all the streets were named after gods and goddesses of the classical world (!) Take that, Mayberry.

Then came the seventies and one of the most popular television series of all times—*Star Trek*. And one of the characters, Dr. Spock, hails from a planet called Vulcan! (Now here's another small-town tourist initiative that makes perfect sense.) In 1995 Vulcan opened a "Star Trek-themed tourist station," which includes a replica of the Starship Enterprise. Since then the town has really thrown itself into the spirit of the series' cult following. They host an annual Star Trek convention called Galaxyfest (or Spock Days). And although they've never been able to get Leonard Nimoy to visit, they've attracted thousands of other freaks and geeks from all over the continent. (And I have nothing but respect for freaks and geeks.) In 2007 they added a "Vulcan Space Adventure" virtual reality game to the attraction, so you can almost believe you are saving the universe.

There's no virtual reality game when we arrive on that sunny day in 2000. But we don't need any help to assume our roles as crew members of the Starship Enterprise. Because they have COSTUMES for us to wear. We all look fabulous in the sleek lines and flattering colours of the crew's uniforms, so we pose for endless photos. We buy Vulcan ears in the gift shop. (I buy extras, sure they'd be a good gift for someone. Or maybe it's just a handy thing to have around the house.) Wearing our ears, and doing all the appropriate hand signals, we pose for more photos in front of the spaceship. We have way too much fun. And that's probably how we got so behind on our schedule . . .

We hit High River on our way back toward Calgary, ostensibly to see some of the murals the town is famous for, but also to eat at some restaurant there that John Paul has heard of. A steak restaurant. More . . . beef. We're not hungry. We're nowhere close to hungry. The mind-body connection between hunger and taking action on that feeling in your stomach has been completely lost. We haven't felt even vaguely peckish for a single instant on this entire trip. How could we?

By now we just respond to the *idea* of food. Almost as though it might be entertaining or interesting to eat, but certainly not necessary.

It would certainly provide an opportunity for more social intercourse of the particular sort enjoyed as one peruses a menu. (Like we haven't had all the intercourse we can handle.) So really it's just a change of scenery that happens to involve food.

By now we're also mindful of the fact that whatever we do we have to do it fast. Stephen and Tyler's plane leaves in three hours, that means we've got one hour to dispense with the food. We order. We wait. And wait. And wait. We tell the server we've got a plane to catch. We wait some more. When the food finally arrives, we've got about seven minutes to suck it back before we gotta hit the road. Really, we should just take some photos of the prettily-arranged platters and leave, but we push the food around our plates for a few minutes and pretend to be interested before we completely give up.

John Paul takes the wheel for this last leg of the journey. We get on Calgary's Deerfoot Trail, normally an efficient north-south artery that leads almost directly to the airport. Not today—it's under construction! Stephen and Tyler resign themselves to missing the flight back to Vancouver.

We get to the airport about ten minutes before the scheduled departure. Tyler and Stephen catapult out of the van; we wave and blow kisses as they charge toward the revolving door.

FROM: Stephen
SENT: Tuesday, July 25, 2000
TO: GALS
SUBJECT: Phew!
Hey you crazy beef-eating kids and cats,

Just wanted to say "thanks" for risking life and limb to get us to the airport last night. We actually made the plane despite the fact that Tyler set off the security alarms. As it turned out, there was a medical emergency on the plane and we didn't leave for another half hour. (An eight-year-old was having an asthma attack—after that run to the flight deck so was I!) If there is a photo radar ticket, we will gladly pay it—depending on how much it is for. Otherwise, we may submit it to Canada Council as a part of our "Canadian Creation" grant application. There has to be a drama coming out of this, n'est-ce pas? It may be called MUSTER!

Hope everyone is recovering from Jerky Withdrawal. I extend again our offer to host you in our Vancouver "B" (i.e., we promise no breakfast) whenever you feel the need of a getaway and can't get to Payne Lake. It would be wonderful to see you all—even if all at once. We have our eye out for neighbourhood game to be shot, stuffed, and mounted—in that order, I think.

Thanks for making the 2nd Annual "Francis the Pig Memorial Stomp Around Alberta Tour" a two-day junket I will never forget. I had chicken for lunch today and chicken for dinner.

Live long and prosper.

xxxxxxxxxxxxxxxxxxxxxxxxxxxxxxxxxxxxxxxxxxxxxxxxxx

Stephen

In these days of post 9-11 airport security they never would have made the flight. Who knew we'd be nostalgic for air travel from the year 2000?

We're dropped off at Patti's where we Edmontonians begin our weary trek home. Next year we won't have this long drive ahead of us at the end of the weekend. Next year, we're starting out in Edmonton and going north. Because next year . . . we are kicking it up on the north by northeast PYROGY TRAIL!!!!

P.S. We're still getting along. Go figure.

Waterton Lakes National Park.

TOUR 2001

GIANT PYROGY

La Corey · Cold Lake
55
41
28
Glendon 660 · Beaver Crossing
881 · Bonnyville
28
Vilna
Smoky Lake · 28
855
29
St. Paul
45 · Andrew 29
855 29
Two Hills
U.F.O. LANDING
2
16
Edmonton
Vegreville
Mundare
2
GIANT EGG
MUNDARE SAUSAGE

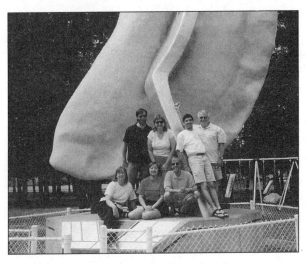

The Gals contemplate their next meal.
PHOTO: PATTI PON

SIX
KICKING IT UP ON THE PYROGY TRAIL

FROM: Patti

DATE: Friday, January 26, 2001

TO: Gals

Subject: buffalo gals wonchya' come out tonight, come out tonight, come out tonight . . .

Buffalo gals wonchya' come out tonight and dance by the light of the moon!!!

Where the hell that came from i don't know!!!! But it felt right . . . there's so many ways to interpret "come out tonight" and "buffalo girls" and the "light of the moon" . . .

Soooooooo thanks to the vision and the foresight of our lovely Mr. Stephen, maybe we should think about setting dates for upcoming trip given that we are such a bunch of jetsetters. Stephen correct me if I'm wrong but are we proposing the weekend of July 7-8 for a trip up North?

It is never too soon to plan for this kids so let's start looking at our calendars and seeing if this can work . . .

Have a happy, happy weekend fellow trekkers. And don't forget . . .

To dance by the light of the MOON.

FROM: Norma
DATE: January 27, 2001
TO: The Gals

I have put the dates on my calendar. Space landing pad, Vegreville Egg. Tour of oil refineries, the sand dunes of Lesser Slave Lake, the healing waters of Lac St. Anne and much more. I can't wait!

Norma

FROM: Conni
DATE: June 29, 2001
TO: Gals
Subject: Buffalo Gals Need to Know . . .
Regarding Accommodations . . .

We figure we could make it to Cold Lake by Saturday night. (Isn't that such a charming name—mind you, my brother's father-in-law hails from Dried Meat Lake.) For your consideration . . .

We found this bed and breakfast 10 minutes east of Cold Lake that sounds quite lovely—(there's an outdoor hot tub, barbecue pit, and she'll cook you anything you want for breakfast.) The catch is, she doesn't have all that many beds. She's got 3 rooms with queen size and ensuite bathrooms, then one with only a double bed. I asked her about a cot or something and then she said she thought she could put a cot in the living room. I tentatively reserved this place so we could have it if we wanted but told the owner I'd get back to her after I talked to colleagues. So that's option one—it's darn cozy. Too cozy?

Option 2 is right on Cold Lake—a bigger, fancier place called Harbour House. Continental breakfast, lots of rooms. Bit more expensive but under 100 bucks per head, I think.

Option 3—we could find a motel. Charm factor zero but lots of beds.

Option 4—go to a rave (in say, Bonnyville) and stay up all night.

Let me know what you think cause I should book asap. Friday night dinner sounds fabu. And yes, Bob, there's huge Ukrainian content in our trip. If them there pyrogies really start to wear on you, we'll try to find a little French village or something. Speaking for myself, I could eat pyrogies for several long years and never tire . . . sigh.

Okay, let me know whatcha think (I'm getting almost as excited as Patti).

XOXOXOOX

FROM: Patti
SENT: June 29/01
I'm not squealing with excitement BUT IT'S PRETTY DAMN CLOSE!!!!!

My vote goes with the cozy B&B. Lookit what happened last year when we went with that, we gots all sorts of animal friends to watch over us as we slept. I'm totally okay with sleeping on the cot in the front room or wherever. Seems to me this would be more in keeping with our past adventures anyhow.

But that's just me.

Patti.

This year we are headed into the land of gi-normous town monuments: giant pyrogies and pysankas and who knows what else we'll encounter. Where did this trend toward "The World's Biggest" start? (Surely the Guinness Book of Records had a hand in this.) Where will it end?

Size does matter, of course. But when I think of being impressed with size . . . perhaps I'll start over. The Empire State Building is big. The Titanic was impressively huge. The giant sequoia trees are truly awe-inspiring. Somehow a giant potato and cheese dumpling doesn't have quite the same capacity to inspire. But it's a great photo op—and a fabulous excuse for a road trip.

There were two innovations in 2001:

1. Though an enthusiastic early supporter of the road trip concept, our friend Brian had thus far been unable to join us as he preferred spending summers in Berlin. (Imagine!) And while we are very, very

sad when Tyler announces that he'll be unable to attend the stomp this year, we are somewhat comforted by the fact that Brian is finally able to make the trek . . .

BRIAN (bon vivant, linguist, Lacombe booster)

Brian is arguably the most glamorous of the Buffalo Gals—a multilingual, widely-travelled opera director. It's potentially really, really useful to have someone who speaks Italian and German and Swedish in your van during a rural Alberta road trip. Still, anyone can see that these road trips have been good for Brian, too. This examination of his roots (and they ain't blonde, I can tell you) provided by our Alberta-centric approach has forced him to face the truth about his personal history. For years Brian's been telling people he was born in Paris and educated in Switzerland. I, for one, suspected this might be untrue when I first met Brian at Red Deer College, especially when I discovered his nearly encyclopedic knowledge of hog breeding.

2. In 2001 another great Buffalo Gals tradition is born: Friday night dinner.

The Calgarians have to travel to us anyway, so we decide to start the party early with a feast of Thaï food.

These additions to the itinerary are a calculated risk. There's always a danger that we'll just have TOOO much fun. Meaning: a little bit too much time in the van together and we might want to kill each other. I wonder (and worry about) what the tipping point might be. Tyler often rhapsodizes about the tenth anniversary week-long Buffalo Gals trip: hiring a small jet to take us from highlight to highlight of the last ten years. I fear it wouldn't end well.

But I digress . . .

The World's Biggest . . .

SEVEN

THE WORLD'S BIGGEST

PRESENT:
Conni, Patti, John Paul, Norma, Stephen, Bob, Kevin, Robert, Brian
ABSENT:
Tyler

Saturday morning we're up bright and early. (Bright and early for us, anyway.) Cause this year we have a deadline. Stephen is directing a play in Rosthern, Saskatchewan. It opens on the Friday night we're meant to start our road trip. He ushers the play (*Quiet in the Land*) into the world, then leaps into his Toyota and drives as far as North Battleford. There's some Walkerton-style water ban on there at the time so he showers with his eyes wide shut before hitting the road to meet us in Vegreville. These are the kind of lengths we go to in order to be together.

We forego our usual diner breakfast extravaganza in favour of take-out from the McDonald's in Sherwood Park, just east of Edmonton.

It's a beautiful, sunny day, so we sit outside with our MacMeals. John Paul, bless his cotton socks, produces champagne from a cooler bag.

We sit in the sunshine, our orange juice topped up with cold, sweet elixir. We toast. Life is so simply good right at this second, I can hardly stand it. We're anticipating fun-fun-fun, sure, but at that moment, it's just about how delighted we feel to be sitting under the crackin' blue sky. Surely the French—or the Italians—have an expression for this. (Didn't Dante say something like "this moment is totally, totally sweet, man"?) I won't speak for anyone else—HAAAAAAHA!—but I feel lucky as hell to be right here, right now.

Time to head east on Highway 16 to Vegreville, Alberta.

The GIANT Ukrainian Easter egg on the edge of town was built as a tribute to the one hundredth anniversary of the RCMP in 1975. At thirty-one feet high, twenty-three feet long, and eighteen feet wide, it is the WORLD'S LARGEST EGG. Made from thirty-five hundred pieces of aluminum, it weighs five thousand pounds. Even at that, it turns in the wind like a weather vane. (Do people actually compete for these world's largest honours? Is the countryside dotted with big whopping eggs that didn't quite make the grade?)

Anyhow, the multicoloured egg is absolutely stunning, glinting in the sun. It doesn't necessarily stir proud feelings about the RCMP, but that's all right. It's stirring, period, and that will have to do. We mill about for awhile, wonder what the anthropologists will make of this monument two hundred thousand years from now when they're unearthing the Egg. They'll assume it's a fertility symbol, I guess. Or an aerodynamically unsound space ship.

The Egg is also the appointed place for meeting Stephen. We're late. He forgives us.

We stow his car in a secure parking lot and then it's time for LUNCH. I mean . . . er . . . culture. At the Ukrainian Pysanka Festival. This is a jolly event that takes place every summer (on the second weekend in July) in this largely Ukrainian community of about four thousand folks. There are crafts, ethnic dancing, and Ukrainian food. We belly up to the concession and order pyrogies and kielbasa and cabbage rolls.

Ukrainian fare is the original comfort food. All the elements—cheese, potatoes, sour cream, bacon, onions—are there. Feeling bad about your life? Have a little dough. In case you've been living on another planet, a pyrogy is a little dumpling filled with potatoes or cheese (or practically anything, really). They're boiled lightly, then (ideally) fried with butter and onions and bacon, and served with a big dollop of sour cream.

Though beef is, of course, always on our minds, this innocent little lump of goodness will be the centrepiece of this year's trip. (Oh why call it a trip; it's a raunchy, gluttonous, romp-stomp.) We gather around a picnic table with our lunch, then join the crowds in the community centre to watch the Ukrainian dancing competitions. We have eaten, we have ogled the egg, we have clapped enthusiastically for the twelve-year-old dance geniuses. Our work here is done.

As we head out of town toward the east, we encounter a shrine to Our Lady of the Highway. We stop and take photos of the Twelve Stations of the Cross. It seems a good omen for the journey ahead. We continue on Highway 16 east for a time, turning north onto Highway 36 before we get as far as Ranfurly. (I only mention this because it's such a lovely name for a town.) Highway 36 jogs up toward Two Hills. (Yes, that's right—in 1999 it was Three Hills. This year . . .)

Somewhere along this lonely secondary highway we encounter a village of people made out of old tires and hay bales. They're dressed in costumes, accessorized to the max, and arranged in tableaux on either side of the long driveway leading up to a small, ordinary farmhouse. It's sort of Edward Scissorhands crossed with Holly Hobby: quaint and creepy all at once. Most everyone wants to stop, so we turn the van around, pull it well off the highway, and wander around this yard taking photos. I certainly wouldn't venture onto anyone's property in the city, but this extraordinary display of creativity and humour seems to invite an audience. We consider knocking on the door and enthusing to our hosts, but that does seem like an imposition. There are vehicles pulled up in front of the house, so we figure they'll come out and chit-chat if they want to. They don't. We tip our hats and leave.

The highway jogs a little to the east and now the town names have a distinctly French–Canadian flavour. We cross a highway that provides access to Brosseau, Duvernay, Beauvallon, though none of these hamlets are on our itinerary. (Eventually we will go through Bonnyville.)

We often take little detours or make unscheduled stops—in the true spirit of road trips—to see if there's still a grain elevator in Hairy Hill, or anything at all in Waskatenau. On this particular afternoon, however, we're highly motivated to get to St. Paul, as that is the site of the UFO LANDING PAD.

Okay, this may not be the WORLD'S BIGGEST, but it was evidently the WORLD'S FIRST. Built in 1967 as a Centennial project, the landing pad has a map of Canada embossed on its backstop, made from stones from all the provinces and territories. ("Welcome to all of Canada, little green men!") Actually the town motto is something like: "We welcome everyone, even from other worlds!"

In 1996, an addition to the Tourist Information Centre adjacent to the launch pad was built to house a "UFO Interpretive Centre." The centre's collection includes actual photographs of UFOs, crop circles and cattle mutilations—we're beside ourselves with excitement. Crop circles! Cattle mutilations! Yippee. Apparently these displays are meant to "educate." Titillate? Educate? What's the diff? And there's more: "The Interpretive Centre will explain various degrees of 'sightings' and show ingenious methods to hoax the public."

Well. Being (mostly) theatre folks, we can probably show *them* a thing or two about hoaxing the public. That's how we make our living, by God. On the other hand, maybe we'll pick up some tips. Then couldn't we write off the expenses from this whole damn trip? But alas—with comedy, family planning, and visiting hours—timing is everything.

We get to St. Paul and the interpretive centre is closed. We're very disappointed. This is where our mythologizing can get us into a bit of hot water. A little healthy anticipation certainly sweetens the slice of life (or pie) but when you're *denied* the experience . . . The van has pulled to a halt but we're still spinning our wheels.

It's about 5 PM on a windy summer day. We desperately want to see evidence of crop circles. Not this trip.

We climb up the stairs to the UFO landing pad. Hard not to feel underwhelmed by this experience. I'm not sure we even took a photo here, which is unusual for us. With all due respect, it's just a flat, empty cement pad, and we're having trouble making the imaginative leap.

Perhaps we'll feel better if we call the UFO HOT LINE. That's: 1-888-SEE-UFOS.

This toll-free number was set up in 1995 to document reports of UFO sightings, cattle mutilations, abductions, and crop circles.

These days, if you phone the hotline, you get the St. Paul Chamber of Commerce and Tourist Information Centre. (I guess the call volume on UFO sightings has gone down a bit in recent years.) On the other hand, this designation—tourist information—makes a certain amount of sense if you're an alien. You're a tourist, for sure, and you'd probably like some information. On the other hand, if you're hoping to open a business in the St. Paul area, it may not be all that encouraging to reach the Alien Welcome Wagon.

The folks at the Chamber of Commerce/Tourist Information/UFO Hotline are still very much on top of the situation. The extremely helpful young woman I spoke to there says that they certainly do investigate UFO sightings, though they tend not to take them too seriously unless several different people report seeing something in the same area. If it's starting to look like a trend, they document the event. (Time of day, appearance of the sky, etc.) As for cattle mutilations, St. Paul has their own self-appointed expert who will go out and investigate these reports. Sort of a Johnny-on-the-spot for analyzing cattle entrails. I assume this is a trade you learn through mentorship and/or trial and error, as I've never seen the course offered at any of the province's community colleges.

We do wonder if maybe St. Paul is Canada's answer to Roswell or something, a location with a high incidence of UFO sightings or other unusual events. (You know, the Gopher Museum principle: we gotta lotta gophers, let's make lemonade.) No such thing—there's been no more UFO sightings in St. Paul than in Ponoka or Picture Butte or

Petawawa. The St. Paul UFO Landing Pad is just a creative idea and one hundred tons of cement. We can't help hoping though, that its very existence will trigger one of the great laws of the universe: If you build it, they will come . . .

The Buffalo Gals stand in a glum little cluster on the landing pad for a few minutes. We wander over and peer in the window of the interpretive centre. Again. There's nothing to do but move on.

We drive for a good long patch this time, through Bonnyville and on to Cold Lake, just inside the Alberta border, and the furthest east we've been on our trips. Cold Lake, Alberta's newest city as of October 2000, is the amalgamation of Grand Centre, Cold Lake and CFB Cold Lake (Medley). We have dinner and pie at a sweet little diner-style restaurant with a great view of the lake, take a stroll on the pier, then it's off to our motel to rest up for the WORLD'S BIGGEST pyrogies and sausages and mushrooms. My goodness—that's a meal right there!

Sunday . . . We're headed to Glendon to see the WORLD'S BIGGEST PYROGY.

Here's the facts, ma'am. At twenty-five feet tall and twelve feet wide, the pyrogy weighs in at an impressive six thousand pounds. It has a great big fork speared through the centre to add an authentic touch. It opened for business in 1993, but you can still get your name engraved on a plaque at the base of the dumpling if you want. We take a LOT of photos in front of this thing. Even more after John Paul points out that the folds of the pyrogy look a little, oh . . . labial? The photos take on a whole new dimension after that, especially once Patti leans too far into a sharp edge and rips the ass out of her pants.

A very nice young man offers to take a photo of us in front of the . . . er . . . monument. We chat him up, of course, and discover that his name is Tyler! (Our beloved and much-missed Tyler is here in spirit.) Our sweet young surrogate invites us to his mom's pyrogy restaurant—more serendipity.

We're not really all that hungry, but we enjoy our delicious little love-dumplings all the same. Tyler reappears in between errands and announces proudly that he's on his way to Edmonton today. (To start a new life?) So are we, we say. We offer to tie him to the roof of the van. He declines graciously and says he has a ticket for the Greyhound, thanks.

On to Vilna, home of the WORLD'S LARGEST MUSHROOMS. Not that we are really hoping for any logic to these choices of iconic foodstuffs, but apparently this monument was inspired by a tradition of mushroom-hunting in this region. The mushrooms are in a funny, scruffy little green space ("Mushroom Park") a couple of blocks off Main Street, and they certainly are big. (The largest of the three is about twenty feet high; together the three mushrooms weigh over eighteen thousand pounds). But the three fungi, which in their original form must have looked like something out of a fairy tale, are now sort of creepy, like broken toys in a deserted house.

I think anyone who lives in the area would probably wonder why we didn't check out the historic barber shop on Main Street or investigate any of the other rich history of the area. Oh well—we have a theme and we're sticking to it.

The visit to Vilna is saved (or at least somewhat redeemed) by the sudden appearance of a local ambassador: an elderly man with a leathery face, twinkly eyes, and a heavy Ukrainian accent. He walks purposefully across the lawn of the little park toward us. (Maybe it was his turn to "man the booth" that day and we caught him on a lunch break.) We tell him we're here to see the mushrooms, and he informs us, with a kind of unassailable authority, that you have to cook mushrooms three times. (At least I think that's what he said.) We smile politely, nod. He repeats the cooking tip, then charges off again.

There. Now that may not have been worth the visit but we're feeling much more satisfied about this pit stop. We get back into the van. It occurs to me that if the people of Vilna are mushroom hunters, surely we must be hunting for stories. And the characters in those stories. We're probably not going to rush off and create an opera based on meeting the old man in the mushroom park, but we're so much happier having had that ten-minute encounter, I can't even tell you.

Our raison d'etre on these trips is comprised of three elements: Are we having a harmonious ranging up to rip-roaringly hilarious time together in the van? Are we seeing some landscape we haven't seen before or seeing some familiar features in a different way? And finally—who do we meet along the way?

Smoky Lake, just a little west of Vilna, is a pretty and prosperous little town with just over one thousand citizens. It's also the Pumpkin Capital of Alberta. Sadly, we're not going to be here for the Great White North Pumpkin Fair and Weigh-off in October, when champion growers haul their enormous pumpkins, squash, and watermelon to town and compete for the big prize.

Still, we can darn well take a photo of ourselves in front of the WORLD'S BIGGEST PUMPKIN (over eight feet in diameter). We drive around looking for a Pumpkin Park. Nope. Maybe the pumpkin is in front of the Smoky Lake sign on the way into town. Nope. We're feeling conspicuous as hell in the Sunday-day-of-rest quiet of Smoky Lake. (We're practically the only vehicle on the road.) We tour the town, toss out desultory quips about lawn ornament displays and about how very nearly sick of pyrogies we might be. And then—someone spots it. The pumpkin! The great pumpkin! It's in a big yard behind a garage, amongst heaps of welding projects and a few half-restored car wrecks. Turns out this is the town's new pumpkin, three feet wider than the old one. Turns out it's not done yet.

Meanwhile, the Greyhound bus has pulled up to a tiny station down the block. One passenger gets out—it's our friend Tyler from the Glendon pyrogy restaurant. We briefly consider yelling a greeting out the window but decide that might just be creepy. We already look like government agents in our big white van. Now what—stalking the locals of Smoky Lake County? Our good humour is somewhat restored as we muse happily about a road trip where we do nothing but follow this young man from town to town. After all, we've often talked about making our own Tyler run ahead of the van.

We stop in Andrew to see the WORLD'S BIGGEST MALLARD DUCK. That's probably all I need to say about that. And now . . . the undisputed highlight of the trip.

Mundare, Alberta is the kind of town I can sort of imagine myself living in if I were ever going to live in a small town again. There are cute houses, big trees, a lovely Main Street with all the essentials: post office, café, and Stawnichy's Meat Processing Plant. Sausage! Kielbasa! Processed meat! YUM. And . . . this town . . . unlike any other place on the planet that I know of, has THE WORLD'S LARGEST SAUSAGE.

This giant (forty-two feet tall) Ukrainian sausage ring, or kielbasa, was built from concrete, steel, and fiberglass with the sponsorship of Stawnichy's Meat Processing Plant. And I'm here to tell you it's a very rude sight. The big red sausage loop has a sort of marbled, veiny texture, and is erected in a little park edged with innocent little flower beds.

We're stunned but appreciative.

PHOTO: BOB ERKAMP

This is the sort of thing that sends our little group into paroxysms. The photo session is endless. The three gals in the group straddling the giant sausage and waving at the camera. Stephen pretending to scale the sausage. Various other rude individuals pretending to hump the sausage. All of us gathered around inside the sausage loop, wearing grave expressions, pointing heavenward. You get the picture.

I guess the question is—are the Mundare folks winking at us or not? I'd say yes. One imagines the committee looking at the drawings for the giant phallic symbol to be built at the centre of town. Imagine the hilarity. I have to assume the whole thing's deliberate, but golly . . . what were they thinking? Well, I guess they were thinking about US.

After the unabashed bawdiness of the Mundare sausage, we really do need to "reel it in." The Basilian Fathers Museum seems just the ticket. The museum is lovely, full of beautiful folk art and religious icons from little country churches. Thus we've sort of bookended the trip with a little moral grounding. Our Lady of the Highway to the Basilian Fathers. Maybe we won't go to hell after all . . .

We have survived another trip. We have had a marvellous time, once again. We don't know it at the time but there's a change coming; soon a small chasm will open up and swallow one of the Gals. But nothing mars our happiness on July 8, 2001. We have seen and conquered some of the world's biggest. We have meandered down the pyrogy trail. All I can say is, this sure as heck ain't Tuscany.

And that's a darn fine thing.

Buffalo Gals about to be crushed by the world's largest Ukrainian Egg.

PHOTO: PATTI PON

EIGHT
ON THE ROAD

You may, at this point in the story, be wondering why in the hell we do this. Cooped up in a van together hurtling toward rusty mushrooms and truly average motel beds. Risking lives and friendships and the goodwill of all we encounter. Why oh why?

Because we are making history.

You see, it's very important to the Buffalo Gals to feel that they're part of a great tradition. Like bridal showers or prison breaks? No, ma'am. Road trips. Hitting the road with some greasy snacks and a good CD in the player is a tradition that dates back to the Middle Ages. (What is Chaucer's Canterbury Tales but one big road trip?) So, ahem; I believe this narrative would be incomplete without some thought-provoking analysis of Great Road Trips of History, thus placing the Buffalo Gals in the proper historical context.

NEAL CASSADY AND JACK KEROUAC: These maniacs took road trips through the American Southwest and Mexico and thus inspired the Beat movement and Kerouac's most famous novel,

On the Road. Of course some of the inspiration may have been drug-induced—these were notoriously stoned expeditions.

The Buffalo Gals are so high on life that we've never once been tempted to enhance or obliterate our experiences with mind-altering substances. Well, except for martinis and red wine. Sure, we sometimes drink before the sun's over the yardarm. And maybe the consumption of spirits is one of the reasons it's so hard to get on the road the next morning. Mind you, I've witnessed a physiological reaction to the over-consumption of beef jerky that is so closely akin to the body's response to heroin that it should probably be studied. I'm afraid to think of what might happen to this crew if they had real drugs . . .

Scene: Buffalo Gals "On The Road"

Tyler: Pass the stuff, man.

Kevin: Pass the map.

Tyler: The stuff, man.

Brian: (*a blood-curdling scream*) The van's moving!

Robert: Duh! We're on a road trip.

Patti: Cool, daddy.

Norma: That's the third time I've seen that sign.

Kevin: Where we going?

Bob: Two Hills.

Tyler: Three Hills! Four Hills!

(Lots of stoner giggling.)

Kevin: Where are we?

Norma: That's the fourth time I've seen that sign.

Tyler: Three Hills! Four Hills!

Brian: Weird, man. We're driving in circles!

Robert: In an empty parking lot.

(Long pause.)

Patti: Cool, daddy.

Oh wait. This is a bit like our regular trips. Well, like I said—we're high on life.

DRIVING MR. ALBERT: Writer Michael Paterniti volunteered to chauffeur a retired pathologist who happened to be in possession of Albert Einstein's brain. They drove from New Jersey to California with the famous grey matter sealed up nicely in a Tupperware container, stored in the trunk. They stopped along the way and visited William Burroughs. They partied in Vegas. Truth way, way weirder than most fiction. I have to say, without any reservations, that the Buffalo Gals have never done anything quite this surreal. But it makes me think . . .

1. Maybe we could drive around with a cooler full of dead gophers in the back of our van. We could use them to do puppet shows at campsites or something.

2. Maybe we could tie obnoxious or useless politicians to our roof rack, along with banners listing their offenses streaming from the back of the van. We could tour the province, slowing down at various points so the good citizens of Alberta could pelt the MLA with tomatoes.

3. Or we could hang our own beef in the back of the van. Disgusting but practical.

Nope. You know, although we've discussed many innovative ideas, some every bit as weird as those listed above, I have a feeling none of them are going to fly. Do we need to have a famous scientist's brain in the back of our vehicle to justify our trips? Absolutely not. Do we need to talk endlessly about the truly bizarre things we could get up to on our road trips if we were so inclined? Absolutely. Besides, we're modest, quiet folks who don't like to draw attention to ourselves. We'd be just as happy sipping ice tea on the back porch with Pappy and Mammy, watching the sunset . . .

BONNIE AND CLYDE: Okay, this is a whole different genre: the crime spree road trip.

Bonnie Parker and Clyde Barrow are probably the most famous advocates of this lifestyle. They cruised around the southern US in the early thirties, robbing small stores, gas stations, and killing a number of people in the process. Viewed as a sort of Romeo and Juliet duo (with a little Robin Hood thrown in), they quickly became folk heroes and have been the subject of various films and books ever since their untimely demise in a roadside ambush.

Being pursued by the law is a whole different kind of travel. It adds a certain urgency to the proceedings that we have never quite felt on our Buffalo Gals tours. Certainly we've been excited to get to various destinations, but we've never been chased out of the last one. Maybe if we tried offending at least one burly redneck in each little town, we'd have to hightail it out of the county, with Bubba in hot pursuit. (Sort of along the lines of the "Keep your city out of my country" edict from the cook-your-own-steak bar in Patricia.)

Mind you, I think we have often been much closer to this scenario than we even knew. Perhaps it was no accident that we were nearly forced off the road by a convoy of gleaming white K-cars after our sacrilegious remarks at the Drumheller Passion Play. (And—wait for it—our dangerous run-in with the Aryan Nation White Supremacists in Caroline, Alberta. That's coming up in 2005.)

Actually now that I think of it—the Buffalo Gals never shy away from doing the right thing—from confronting evil and intolerance—even if it means being chased down a dirt road by angry ranchers. Hmmm . . . I just thought I'd try out that "Buffalo Gals On the Road for Justice" version of events. Run it by y'all. You know—hoist it up the flagpole to see if anyone salutes. Not so much. But you have to admit it would be a whole different kind of vacation.

Of course one has to take into account the personalities involved. While a few of us Buffalo Gals have from time to time had a kind of marginal, starving artist-style existence, none of us have yet robbed a liquor store in order to pay the rent. No, if one of our

Buffalo Gals road trips turned into a crime spree, it would probably be more along the lines of Thelma and Louise . . .

THELMA AND LOUISE: This 1991 movie is the story of two gal pals, Thelma and Louise, who set out innocently enough on a girly-girl road trip. Then they accidentally murder a man, and plus some other bad stuff happens; finally they drive off a cliff and plunge to their deaths. The thing here is, unlike Bonnie and Clyde, Thelma and Louise didn't set out to make trouble—it's just that one thing sort of led to another.

It's sooooo easy to see how that could happen on one of our road trips. Take, for instance, the seemingly innocent search for the World's Largest Pumpkin in Smoky Lake, Alberta. There we are, we've found the partially completed pumpkin, but it's behind a steel-link fence. Say someone—Kevin, for instance—really, really wanted to touch the pumpkin. We do try to accommodate individual itches and quirks and heartfelt desires on these road trips, so we hoist Kevin over the fence so he can fondle the big orange gourd. (He's never been the same since he donned the Clem T. Gofur head.)

Only, what if Kevin catches his pants on the fence and rips them wide open? That's a public indecency charge just waiting to happen. (Patti only just missed being arrested after her pyrogy-pant-ripping incident.) The rest of the Gals rush to a nearby diner, order a burger, and argue about whether or not we should bail Kevin out of the hoosegow. Next thing you know, he's hung himself with his shoelaces. Tragic.

Or . . . there's a guard dog in the compound with the great pumpkin and Kevin beans him with a tire iron and the dog dies and the owner calls the police and we know we have to get out of town and fast. Kevin takes too much time climbing back over the fence so we leave him there cause we can hear the police siren. We have no choice—the Smoky Lake constabulary is on the way! (I volunteer to explain all of this to Kevin's mother.) Anyway, you can see how something entirely innocent could turn tragic. We're just really, really lucky we've escaped this sort of mishap thus far.

EARLY EXPLORERS: Now these guys knew their road trip shit. David Thompson and Alexander Mackenzie and Simon Fraser—to name but a few—were all highly motivated to reach their destinations. But in true road trip spirit, they also discovered a lot of other things along the way. And man, they were brave. Crazy, even. Charting the unknown wilderness for queen and country. Writing the bloody maps, suffering terribly in the process—or actually dying.

What we share with these guys is the fortitude to continue looking for something that just may not exist, and the good humour to deal with the ensuing disappointment. How is our quest to find the perfect pyrogy or the great pumpkin really any different than the search for the Northwest Passage? (I mean, in essence.) There's the little matter of scale and sheer difficulty, of course, but there's nobility in all these pursuits. Would we die in search of the pyrogy or the pumpkin? Impossible to say. But then we're not bucking to have a river system or a university named after us, either.

Many of these "brave new world" episodes didn't end so heroically, anyway. For instance, many settlers seem to have had a particularly hard time on their road trips. In order to present a balanced view of history and, frankly, as a cautionary tale, I feel I really must mention . . .

THE DONNER PARTY: This group of eighty-seven California-bound American settlers became snowbound in the Sierra Nevada in the winter of 1846–1847. They slaughtered their oxen but it wasn't quite enough grub to feed the group. Hunger and the worst of winter (raging blizzards and the like) took a further toll. Eventually some of them resorted to cannibalism in order to survive. Of the original pioneers, thirty-nine died and forty-eight survived.

Hmmm. Perhaps the Buffalo Gals will think twice before they attempt a winter road trip. I mean, we've been stranded without food on a perfectly lovely summer day, and let me tell you—it was not a good scene. (2004: the Apocalypse Cow Tour. Somewhere around Vauxhall it looked like we wouldn't be able to have lunch. Bob was really, really not happy. And I thought I saw a kind of maniacal glint in his eye when someone suggested roasting a bit of road kill on the radiator of the van. He actually licked his lips when I pretended to gnaw on my own pink, meaty forearm. Ordinarily I would vouch for the character of the Buffalo Gals under any circumstances, but I don't know—they do without food for a couple of hours and something wicked this way comes.)

CAROL WHO I WENT TO HIGH SCHOOL WITH: Carol was born in the back of a 1954 International Harvester half-ton truck. Her mother, having already easily birthed a couple of strapping lads, got a tad nonchalant about the timing of the drive from their farm to the hospital, so they had to make an unscheduled stop by the side of a gravel road. I'd say that's pretty much in the spirit of road trips. And Carol's a much better souvenir than a T-shirt from the gift shop at Head-Smashed-In.

ALAN WHO I WENT TO UNIVERSITY WITH: I don't normally include family outings under the road trip banner, but Alan's family trip to Disneyland is just too sad not to include. Plus, I know there's probably some deep and abiding wisdom therein . . .

The facts are as follows: One fine day in the mid-seventies, Alan's parents decided to take the whole family—Alan and two brothers—on a trip to Disneyland. They started out from Kelowna, BC in the station wagon, and the expected mayhem kicked in: three brothers squabbling constantly. Alan's dad kept warning that he would turn the car around and go right back home if the kids didn't behave. Just north of Anaheim, California, Alan's dad did something shocking. (In the parenting books it's what they call "following through.") Forty-five minutes from Nirvana—the epicentre of fun, the promised land for kids everywhere—Alan's dad pulled a U-turn on the I-5 and headed back to Kelowna. Fifteen hours of intermittent sobbing and sullen silence ensued. Crazy, huh? Cruel, even? Dunno. I can't imagine spending hours and hours in a station wagon with three obnoxious prepubescent boys, maybe I'd snap too. Oh hang on, sometimes that's exactly what it feels like on our road trips.

Which brings me to the matter of discipline in the van. One of these times, if I can ever wrestle the wheel away from one of the control freaks who like to hog all the driving on our trips, I might take the opportunity to "follow through" on some threats. I believe a little tough love may be required on the matters of a) bad puns, b) monopolizing the treat bag or the Culture section of the *Globe and Mail*, and c) PaSu-whining. "Stop it this instant or we're heading back to Red Deer," I'll say sternly.

THE ADVENTURES OF PRISCILLA, QUEEN OF THE DESERT: Trust the Aussies to lead the way. This 1994 smash hit was about two drag queens and a transsexual travelling across the desert in a lavender bus to perform a drag show at a resort in Alice Springs. The bus breaks down, hilarity ensues, it all turns out in the end . . .

We referenced this movie a lot in the first couple of years of the trip; it is undoubtedly the reason we decorated the van in 2000. (We still muse about attaching long, pink streamers to the van, and towing a fleet of armchairs attached to a flatbed trailer so we can enjoy the fresh air.) But I think the parallel goes a bit deeper than that. Part of the charm of the movie lies in the contrast between the rugged Australian outback and the fruity splendour of the drag queens. Though none of us gals are drag queens, we often feel like outsiders as we travel the highways of our own province.

OTHER GREAT ROAD TRIPS: There are a million great road trip movies; there are a lot of great books about piling into the Buick or loading up the wagon or saddling the horses. What do we all have in common?

You decide to go somewhere. You pretty much agree that the journey is much more important than the destination. (A possible exception to this rule would be a trip into town to give birth to a baby.) But you do have some articulated goals or a loose agenda to guide your meandering. Some unexpected things occur, and you do your best to go with the flow or roll with the punches. You may eat things that aren't good for you. You hope to get along with the other people in the vehicle (the car, the bus, the van, the Red River cart). I think that about covers it. That certainly describes the Buffalo Gals tours.

How is the Buffalo Gals touring outfit *different* from the above-noted examples?

I think that gives rise to the real question: How is a pilgrimage different from a road trip?

A religious pilgrimage tends to have some soul-improving motives; it consists of a journey to some religiously significant location (like a shrine). I think the idea is that the pilgrim gets as much out of the striving, the possible hardship encountered in getting to the destination, as he or she gets out of savouring the journey's end. Well, so far that all sounds just like us—one person's Santiago de Compostela is another person's Fay Wray fountain, right?

I say, if you've gone to a certain amount of trouble to reach a very specific location (crawling up stone steps on your hands and knees, wearing unflattering sackcloth, going without sustenance for two hours), and you feel edified or improved once you arrive, your road trip qualifies as a pilgrimage. After all, what were we doing in Red Deer, kneeling respectfully by the statue of Francis the Pig? We were paying tribute to an inspiring individual, marvelling at the spirit of Francis, and hoping for a little of that death-cheating gusto in our own lives; we were MAKING A PILGRIMAGE.

There's been some suggestion that the whole notion of pilgrimage has been downgraded somewhat with the advent of such popular jaunts as going to PEI to touch Lucy Maude Montgomery's chamber pot or to Memphis to see Elvis's coffee mug. I think we can probably lay some of the blame for this at John Wayne's door. In one of his cowboy personas his shtick is as follows: he sort of whips out his pistol hand, points an index finger, and drawls: "How ya doin' pilgrim?" How can you maintain your pilgrim poker-face after that sacrilege?

Anyhow. I'm glad we've had this little chat before going on to Buffalo Gals, 2002 wherein several of the Buffalo Gals drag the other Gals on a PILGRIMAGE to the communities from whence they sprang.

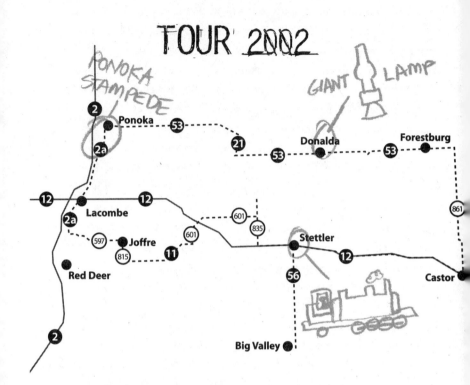

Moments before our departure on the Stettler steam train excursion.
PHOTO: BOB ERKAMP

NINE
YOUR ROOTS ARE SHOWING

PRESENT:
Brian, Robert, Conni, Patti, Norma, Bob
ABSENT:
Stephen, Tyler, Kevin, John Paul

One of the things that makes the Buffalo Gals work as a concept is our regional diversity. Stephen hails from Brampton; he did a master's degree and ran a theatre in Edmonton, but now lives in Vancouver. His partner Tyler, son of an itinerant General Motors executive, has lived absolutely everywhere clear across the country. Kevin's an Ontario boy, Bob's from Montreal. Norma grew up in Vancouver, John Paul was born and raised south of the border. Of course we've also drawn heavily on the heartland of Alberta for our Buffalo Gals membership. My hometown (Ponoka) is in central Alberta, and I have family sprinkled here and there all over the province. Brian was born and raised in Lacombe. Patti, though born and raised in Calgary, has family ties to the small town of Castor, and Robert was born in Camrose, not that far from Castor.

I thought it was inevitable that we'd do a Roots trip with the Buffalo Gals, but some members of our little troupe seem less than enthusiastic about seeing the parking lot of Ponoka Composite High School, where so much of my character was formed. Maybe that's why we had such a poor turnout on this trip.

Stephen and Tyler were so busy driving a barge in France that they declined to join us. Actually they got back from their fabulous European holiday about thirty-six hours before they would have had to get right back on a plane to join us. They were just too darn tired to make the scene. I think this shows an astonishing lack of commitment, but it may be that Stephen was still exhausted from driving all night to meet us for the 2001 trip. Kevin was working as a musical director on some show in Calgary. Pffff!

The other casualty of the Buffalo Gals 2002 Tour was John Paul. Sometime during the spring of 2002, he and one of our other Gals had a falling-out. The end of a friendship is one of those hopelessly sad things in life which need not be examined in any forensic detail here. This unexpected development does, however, give us another sort of problem.

Once it becomes clear that John Paul will not be joining us in 2002, we have an empty place on the tour. A *new* spot, temporary absences notwithstanding.

Now you'll probably think I'm exaggerating if I say there has been considerable jockeying for position, lobbying for inclusion, and just plain old heavy-handed hinting about being invited to be a Buffalo Gal. Mostly we've been quite firm that we'd only ever have as many people as could comfortably (or reasonably) fit in a van. (Thus the luggage restrictions of later years.) Since none of us had any desire to be part of a road trip convoy, as has also been suggested to us, we've been fairly safe from aggressive membership inquiries.

Still, the whole thing has been quite astonishingly political. We decide, in that sort of group dither-ish way, apparently communicating by telepathy or divine intuition since we never actually talked about it, that we just wouldn't deal with the issue of the absent member. It seemed a bit harsh to be putting up posters advertising a seat on the tour. So we launch the trip with our smaller crew: *six* Buffalo Gals. Who needs to rent a hotel? We could sleep in the van.

Speaking of accommodations—and politics—we do briefly consider staying in the former home of one of our premiers: Don Getty. Widely acknowledged as one of our less distinguished leaders, Getty is mostly remembered as a professional football player. At one point during his political career he was parachuted into the riding around Stettler, where he built a palatial country house, now rented out to tourists. It sounded like it might be right up our alley, to spend the night pottering around in an ex-premier's house, perhaps staging a little political satire (with music) to while away the hours. But it was too rich for our blood.

Since Lacombe is roughly equidistant from Edmonton and Calgary, we agree to meet there at Brian's ancestral home.

Friendly competition and/or open hostility between neighbouring municipalities is a long-standing tradition. The foolish rivalry between Edmonton and Calgary still seems to have teeth, especially during hockey and football season. (Gee, that's nearly twelve months of the year.) The rivalry between Ponoka and Lacombe (please refer to your map to see the terrifying proximity of these two burgs) exists mostly in the minds of Brian and myself. I must confess that I often get the short end of the stick in this competition, and that's because of one simple fact, something completely out of my control. An accident of fate and government planning. Since I can't live this down I must simply aim to rise above the given circumstances and ignore Brian's childish taunts. You see . . .

During the years I was growing up, Ponoka was the site of the largest mental hospital in the province. I was ten years old before I was made aware of the cruel hilarity arising from this fact. My Calgary cousin filled me in—we were having a disagreement about something, and this information was his trump card. I was devastated to hear the witticisms inspired by our town's largest employer. ("I'm from Ponoka. Out on a weekend pass?" Arrrrh—ha-ha! And so on.)

By comparison, Lacombe has the Dominion Experimental Farm, AKA home of the Lacombe Hog, a superior breed of pig developed at the Lacombe Research Station. This pig is almost as famous as Francis, a fact you may be unaware of unless you run in those circles. (Pig Circles? Pork Loops?) You'd think over the long years of my friendship with Brian I'd be able to get more mileage out of pigs and experiments on pigs and the like, but the joke never really gets any traction. But speaking of traction . . .

July 1, 2002

We forego the Friday dinner this year and instead meet in Lacombe early Saturday, borrow Brian's parents' van (since our numbers are small), and hit the road. But not before we've given Lacombe its due. We herd the van down the historic Main Street—very nicely restored, I admit grudgingly. Main Street also has something found only in small towns these days, it seems: The Family Department Store. (Eatons should qualify, I suppose, but it doesn't seem quite the same.) The Lacombe version is Kanngiesser's, the Ponoka version is Wedin's.

We drive past the Experimental Farm. "Oh, like, big whup," I mutter. Brian punches me. (We've now regressed to age fourteen, just this side of food fights and "I know you are, but what am I?") We slowly cruise past a couple schools, imagining tender scenes from Brian's youth. The playgrounds are deserted now of course, on this beginning-of-summer weekend, but we all enjoy envisioning little Brian being shoved and taunted by the farm kids who may not have appreciated his precocious verbal skills and vast knowledge of Broadway musicals. Brian wants to show us the *real* theatre attached to his high school. (Sorry, this is another sore point. In Ponoka they had a few town meetings about building a real performance space, but it came to nothing. Sigh. Hockey-hockey-hockey.) But none of us really want to see the site of Brian's former theatrical triumphs. There's a strong consensus that we instead should see . . .

. . . the birthplace of Suzie Pasadena, the biggest slut in Brian's class. He has so often dropped her name into conversation all these years that she's taken on iconic status as the big über-easy, the girl with too many curls, the village mattress. We herd the van past a small, beige bungalow. Norma wants to take photos. We stop her. Patti wants to knock on the door and ask how things turned out for Suzie. We nip that in the bud too. Meanwhile Brian tells us a few more x-rated anecdotes about Suzie. Wow, they even have badder girls in Lacombe than in Ponoka. I never guessed we'd lose *that* competition.

There's also just no denying that Lacombe is now twice the size of Ponoka, partly because it's a bit of a bedroom community for the city of Red Deer, just twenty minutes further south. Just twenty minutes to the north, we'll find *my* old hometown. I change into a crisp white blouse, take the mic at the front of the van and start the tour . . .

We take the little secondary highway (2A North) that runs parallel to the main highway and is considerably more picturesque. It's pretty and winding; it's also littered with pop cans, plastic grocery bags, and memories. I provide a run-on commentary. A guy I went to high school with died after driving his car into that highway divider the people on that farm over there have burned down two houses in ten years oh look a geodesic dome everybody thought they were total freaks when they built that see there I used to go to that little campsite over there to neck with my high school sweetheart hee hee. And—and—and—

I realize that the other Gals seem to have slipped into a coma. I give up on the adolescent anecdotage—only temporarily—and expend my energies working the Buffalo Gals into a rodeo frenzy. After all, we are headed for the BIGGEST SIX DAY RODEO IN ALBERTA. Repeat after me: YEEEE-HAA! One more time! Take *that*, Lacombe Hog!

If you like rodeos, you won't want to miss the Ponoka Stampede, honest. It's roughly the same calibre of competition as the world-famous Calgary Stampede, only the whole experience is cozier. The grandstand's smaller, you're closer to the action; the midway's sort of cute rather than imposing, and it's easier to get to the grounds from your hotel. Overall, I think it's just a more intimate experience than the Calgary Stampede. (An "intimate" rodeo, now I've really gone too far.)

We get a seat in the grandstand and watch the Saturday afternoon show: barrel racing, bull riding, steer wrestling. It's not for the faint of heart, admittedly. (Considerably more shocking than stuffed gophers, let me tell you.) I spot a celebrity—it's Miss Ponoka Stampede! She wears very tight jeans and a nifty headdress: her tiara is snugged into the band of her cowboy hat, and it all seems to be attached to a long fall of obviously fake hair, trailing down her back. Maybe she's bald under all that. I lie to the other Gals, telling them that of course I took my turn as Miss Ponoka Stampede. They look skeptical, Brian even giggles. I revise: No, actually I was Miss Alberta Beef. Patti and Norma nod (admiringly?) but Robert blows it, saying innocently that this is the first time he's heard of this. Open guffawing. Truly petulant now, I almost insist that I was runner-up for Ponoka Ice Carnival Queen, but at the last minute I opt for the truth: I was class historian at my high school graduation ceremony.

And that, my friends, is why I was destined to write a history of our road trips.

Suddenly the heavens open up and it pours. We retreat to the nearby beer tent and get a pitcher of draft. The sun comes out almost immediately, and we watch the rest of the show whilst sipping suds.

We should leave town immediately following the grandstand show, as we have many miles to go before we sleep. But I hijack the van and continue narrating "My Ponoka Story—Figure Skates and Pussy Willows." Oh no, wait—"Half-Tons and Heifers." Or . . . I expect that's quite another book. Still, we do drive past a) my high school, and b) the former site of Poor Gordie's Burger Bar, and c) the place just north of town where the boys used to race the quarter mile. My old haunts are a) deserted; b) torn down, in the case of Poor Gordie's; and c) devoid of feeling or atmosphere. While I have, of course, been home many times since high school, it's funny-odd seeing the tour from the Buffalo Gals perspective.

Am I looking for some sign that I was here? I can somehow under-stand why people climb up on overpasses and spray paint GRAD '86. It's illegal, unsightly, without a hint of poetry or imagination or artfulness. But for that one, shining, drunken moment—Trevor or

Jason stretched out over the precipice doing the deed while Biff and Carla and Nick hold his legs—they know this night belongs to them alone. *They* are the ones who will change the world.

Maybe I'm really looking for some indication of how much of my high-school self remains. Yes, I know, I know—in some ways we all retain an aspect of the child inside—that quivering mess of an adolescent, that joyful toddler. Perhaps this is better explained in the context of a long-running gag between Brian and me.

See, curiously enough, Brian can just as easily channel 'good old boy' as cosmopolitan bon vivant. His social circles are left-leaning, liberal, and artsy, and yet, every once in a while Brian slips into some seventy-five-year-old version of himself in an alternative universe, sipping coffee at the local Co-op—making pronouncements about buddy-what's-his-name who should get a job or the young offender who should be hung up by his cojones instead getting a free ride courtesy of the taxpayers. And on and on in this vein. This highly entertaining display of political incorrectness can usually be managed by leaning over and pretending to adjust an errant label at the back of Brian's shirt. We call it "tucking in the Lacombe." Well, that's unless I'm in exactly the same mood for some reason, channelling Ethel the head waitress at the Royal Hotel in Ponoka. Then we could be lost to the world for hours.

I have a tradition for maintaining sanity in rehearsals which may in fact derive from my roots, or the values instilled by my upbringing. Rehearsing a new play is a bit of a pressure cooker, to say the least. It's easy to start obsessing, to be pitched into despair because you just can't figure out how to solve the ending, or because that one actor isn't quite what you'd imagined. One can easily get to a point, about thirteen days, five hours and twenty minutes into the process, when you think the top of your head might blow off from thinking too hard. Around about that time I try to have what I call a "we're not shipping serum to the Congo" day. Meaning: this is important, sure, but it's not THAT important. Which is not to denigrate the importance of art or my passion for storytelling. It's just a way of gaining a little perspective. Maybe that's the Ponoka in me . . .

Donalda, Alberta, east of Ponoka, is the birthplace of another famous Albertan blonde—Tricia Helfer, who starred in the television series Battlestar Galactica. It's also home to the World's Largest Oil Lamp. (Aha—and you thought we were done with all that.) The lamp is, well, it's big all right. The best part, just beyond the lamp, is that the landscape suddenly falls away to reveal some hoodoos. They're not as dramatic as the Drumheller versions, far to the south; they're more like a promising echo of the real thing, but a delightful surprise all the same.

A village of nearly three hundred people, Donalda has a lovely, wide Main Street with trees planted down the middle. The oil lamp museum is closed, but we have a look in the antique store, having already noted that there's a little tea shop, "The Nutcracker Suite," across the street. (Saskatoon pie!) But while we're nosing around in the antique store, the Nutcracker Suite closes. Not to be deterred, Robert and I peer through the window, and then knock on the door until the bewildered owner finally appears from the back. We ask her nicely if she'd consider reopening and she agrees. (This is hunting and gathering, Buffalo Gals-style.) We make it worth her while. Tea, coffee, and saskatoon berry ice cream sundaes are consumed; many jars of jam and saskatoon syrup are purchased. We Buffalo Gals may have our lapses, but we got the retail thing down pat.

We proceed east through Forestburg and pick up Highway 36 South. Soon we'll be in Castor. After Patti's grandfather finished working on the railroad, he and his brother opened a restaurant here called The Blue Bird Café. Patti's grandmother came from China to join the family, but died young after the birth of her ninth child. (She's buried in the Castor Cemetery.) Meanwhile, a young W.O. Mitchell had taken a job as a school principal in town. After meeting Patti's grandfather, who was now coping with nine kids as a single parent as well as running a restaurant, Mitchell took in two of the children and basically raised them. Thus began a long association between W.O. Mitchell and Patti's family. Years later, when Patti's mother passed away, W.O. Mitchell's son Hugh did the eulogy.

In our usual style, we get to town after they've pretty much rolled up the sidewalks. We speculate, under the leadership of Patti, about where the family café might have been located. We settle on a pale blue building on Main Street. "The Blue Bird Café" is such a pretty and hopeful name. We think of the dreams this family must have had: moving to Canada, raising children, growing a business. Most important, the events that took place here all those years ago led directly to Patti being in our midst. And for that we are eternally grateful.

We may be too late to tour the local hardware store, but it's never too late to visit the town monument. And let me tell you—we've been looking forward to this for weeks. Cause the town's mascot is a beaver. (Castor = beaver en Francais.) Perhaps even the WORLD'S LARGEST BEAVER. We are nearly apoplectic with anticipation. Especially since the beaver is named Patti. I'm hoping I don't have to elaborate—given what you now know about the extremely juvenile level of humour in this crew—about the kind of hilarity that ensues when we discover that not only is this beaver very large, but that it's also rusty, discoloured, and well, sort of sad-looking. We take a few photos, crack a few tasteless jokes, and then trundle back to the van. We've had our fun, such as it is, and it's time to push on to Stettler.

As of 2008, there's no mention of the beaver on the town's website. There is, however, a great slide show of photos taken around the area. The list of views includes: Cenotaph, Castor Creek, Coulees, Badlands, Hoarfrost, and my personal favourite: Moonrise@Castor Creek Donut.

Now we gotta sleep and eat. I mean eat and sleep. Because we're resting up for tomorrow and the big TRAIN TRIP!

Okay, hang on. I'm just going to admit I'm drawing a blank here about our Saturday night. Thought I'd consult my colleagues. Of course this leads to a lot more input than I actually wanted . . .

BRIAN WEIGHS IN: All I remember is lots of beef. The lantern museum in Donalda was closed. We went to that place and had saskatoon sundaes. When we left it was kind of a mixture of storm clouds and sunlight. There was pretty light over the coulees. (The sun was going down over the coulees?) You think we went to Castor after that? No, I don't think we went to Castor on this trip. I don't remember that, I remember the light in the sky.

We went to Buffalo Lake and then Donalda. In Stettler . . . we stayed at some motel. We had a drink at the Legion. We had steak.

We nearly ran out of gas on the way home, had to fill up in Blackfalds cause we didn't think we'd make it to Lacombe.

PATTI WEIGHS IN: Stettler itself was the most uneventful part of the trip. We stayed in a Best Western with king-size beds that coulda been anywhere, and I believe that while we threatened to go to the Legion we didn't. We ended up trying to find a dining spot near the hotel, and it turned out to be one of those classic small-town pizza places owned by a Greek family. Amazing how many of those we've hit over the years.

We went through some campsite because we were looking for Don Getty's house and had actually overshot. It seemed like a good idea at the time to take a tour through the campground. Maybe we stopped there to ask about the Don Getty house . . . ?

The train trip was all about the "Train Robbery," and Norma and Bob reminiscing about oldee tymeeeee songs and performances that some of our theatre friends have witnessed and participated in over the years. Remember that singing duo who were on board doing the singalong? Wasn't Brian correcting them on some of the lyrics since he knew every single one of the songs they sang?!?!

The Alberta Prairie Railway
We're signed up for a ride on a vintage steam-powered train that goes from Stettler to Big Valley and back again. Big, big fun. Boarding takes place at 10:30 AM Sunday morning, the train departs at 11 AM. The train is beautifully restored—it looks like something out of a movie. All aboard!

We take our assigned seats. The train slowly picks up speed but then settles in at what feels like about fifty kilometres an hour. We're moving at an amble down a track that cuts through rolling fields and stands of poplar. On one leisurely turn there's a cluster of Alberta rose bushes in full bloom—so close I could lean out the train window and pick a flower if only my friends would just hold my legs. We see a couple of deer leap off the track and into the woods. A coyote stands stock still at the edge of a field. For much of the trip you can stare off in any direction and pretend it's a hundred years ago. Ahh, the pleasures of a slow train headed for nowhere particularly important . . .

The main event occurs mid-trip. The train slows down even more, the squealing brakes finally bringing us to a complete stop. We have an inkling of what's coming but pretend to be mystified for the benefit of the wide-eyed kids in the next row. If you stick your head out the window, you can see them coming in the distance: three or four men wearing long duster coats and ominous robber-bandanas that cover their faces, riding alongside the train on huge, powerful horses.

Our host for this train trip, a man dressed as Gabriel Dumont, informs us that the train is under attack by the notorious Bolton Gang. Not to worry—Gabriel's on the case. But just then a couple of the robbers slide off their horses and burst into our car. They move down the aisle—it's a holdup! Grown-ups, in on the joke, throw toonies and five dollar bills in the proffered pouches. (The proceeds are later donated to charity.) But the real fun is watching the kids, open-mouthed with awe. The whole performance is pitched perfectly to seem real enough to be engaging, but never truly frightening. And I can't help thinking what a great gig this must be for a few local ranchers, to saddle up their horses and "rob a train" every few days. What a hoot. The robbers finish their dirty work and disembark. But our hero Gabriel Dumont is waiting for them. There's a well-choreographed gunfight in the tall grass of the field beside the train. Gabriel is triumphant—we can carry on to Big Valley—and lunch!

Big Valley is a tiny village which seems to exist purely for our pleasure. A little loop of shops around a boardwalk sells ice cream and folk art and souvenirs. Main Street leads to a community hall where the good people of Big Valley are going to serve us a roast beef dinner. After being fed and watered, we wander up the hill to see a tiny, blue, wooden church. We buy delicious fudge at the fudge shop, ostensibly for the ride home, but gobble it up long before we're due to board the train.

There's just no avoiding the anticlimactic feel of the trip back to Stettler, but our hosts try to take off the edge with non-stop musical entertainment. The singing duo who roam the train cars, with their Roaring Twenties songbook, banjo, and bad/goofy humour, inspire a spate of theatre anecdotes. And that's how we spend our time on the way back, trading tales, lulled by the gentle rhythms of our slow train.

Home again, home again, jiggedy jig. We make a small detour so Brian can see the newly-constructed gas plant at Joffre. We nearly run out of gas between there and Lacombe—I'm actually just surprised this hasn't happened to us before now. We settle our bills over a pint in the Lacombe Hotel.

I notice a curious thing on this trip. For the first time, in my mind anyway, the big scheduled events—the Stampede, the train trip—have been a bit underwhelming. It's odd. The Stampede was just as it should have been. The train trip was all you could expect—there was food, music, theatre, scenery—I don't know what else they could possibly lay on for our benefit. Maybe it didn't seem quite as jolly due to our smaller numbers. But no, the company's as grand as usual, though just a shade more subdued. After all, with this freelancing, freewheeling crew, there are bound to be times when people just can't make it.

Of course, it could be that the trip won't always be a priority for everyone. After all, Stephen and Tyler have to come from Vancouver now, a huge expense racked-up on top of the exorbitant cost of our forty-eight-hour binges. Maybe the day will come when they just can't justify it. Kevin is often unavailable for the trip. It's perfectly understandable, as a freelance artist you take the work when it comes. Maybe we'll never have a full complement of Gals again—maybe it'll never again be like that first glorious trip. And what if we just run out of things to see? Well, things that meet our exacting standards of kitschy weirdness, anyway.

That's it—maybe 2002 was a little short on cheesiness. Other than the beaver in Castor, there just wasn't enough big, foolish fromage.

Where was the giant sausage? The hay-bale village? And where was our sacrilegious component? We'll certainly bear these requirements in mind for next year. Of course we could always just revert to a simpler model for hanging out together. We could meet in Calgary, have a meal or two, see a play, then debrief over red wine. We'd be together, we'd have some laughs, surely that would serve the same purpose. And yet . . .

That really, really would not be anything close to the same. It's about touring remote corners of Alberta—and spending hours and hours together in the van. It's about moving heaven and earth to fit this into our schedules. It's about—it's about—I'm hyperventilating now. I can't help myself; I just worry, that's all. I worry that we've had more than our share of fun and that to enjoy any more hilarity and beauty would just be greedy. Maybe it's time to recognize that we've had our portion of joy, our pounds of cow flesh and that to persist in this folly—all these strong personalities trapped in the van together, ignoring whatever tensions may develop, getting restless, or irritated, even bored—is to invite disaster.

Well darn it, when the day finally comes that we have to stop doing this, I think we should go out with a bang. I think we should rent a van and drive it off the big cliff at Head-Smashed-In Buffalo Jump, half of us yelling whoo-hoo and the other half with their mouths stuffed full of jerky!

But I don't think we're there yet. You see, I realize part of what distinguishes our trip from other road trips is our pig-headed longevity. Unless you count annual family adventures in the station wagon—and I don't cause families are stuck together and have no choice but to find a way to pass the time while the kids grow up—then I think we're headed for some kind of record, and it's only year four. Imagine if we made it even one more year—to the FIFTH ANNUAL BUFFALO GALS ROMP AND STOMP.

On the first weekend of March in 2003, about half of us gather at a theatre festival in Calgary. We have a meeting about Buffalo Gals. After hours of tense negotiation (or ten minutes and a coin toss), we decide that a trip to the Crowsnest Pass will be our 2003 tour.

There's still one more important matter to be settled—we have a spot left on the tour.

We decide to conduct province-wide auditions; candidates will be asked to prepare a classical piece, a dance number, followed by an improvised scene with one of us sitting on the audition panel, simulating conditions in the van. The latter will be an important test of the candidate's flexibility and overall suitability. In short, it's Canadian Road Trip Idol. Auditions are scheduled for Edmonton, Calgary, Red Deer and Tierra del Fuego. We each agree to take turns on the panel. I agree to send sensitive letters to disappointed applicants. "You may be someone else's perfect Buffalo Gal, just not ours . . ." And so on.

Suddenly we're all just overwhelmed by the real potential for this to go sideways. What if some wide-eyed acolyte makes a perfectly good case for herself, professing a love of beef and badinage, then we find out she doesn't like shopping or bacon? It's just really difficult to test for and verify all the right qualities in a travel companion. Overwhelmed by politics and other painful realities, we decide nothing. Or rather, to do nothing.

Then deep into May, the time for crop seeding and theatre season announcements, tragedy strikes. Neither Bob nor Kevin can join us this year. We wonder if we should entertain the possibility of a one-time-only replacement Gal, just for this trip. I know just the man for the job, my bosom pal Richard.

RICHARD (replacement Gal, recreation director, glee club alumnus)
Richard's natural tendency toward grim forbearance can be a welcome antidote to the prevailing mood of excitement and sickly Mary Poppins-like enthusiasm in the van. Sometimes we really do need someone to take us down a peg with some good old-fashioned central Albertan skepticism. As in:

Foreigner: It is a beautiful day, no?

Central Albertan: (reluctantly) Uh-huh. (with grim certainty) We'll pay for it later, though.

Richard comes from an extremely musical family. (Just this side of the Von Trapps, I tell you. They actually gather around the piano at Christmas and warble together as a family after every meal—these guys make the Waltons look like dysfunctional thugs.) Given all that, do you think he might collaborate with Kevin on composing and orchestrating our long-awaited Buffalo Gals theme song? No, apparently not.

Richard accepts the invitation to be a replacement Gal with the understanding (the suspicion?) that he may be cruelly ousted after one trip—relegated to joining the crowds of people who gather along major roadways in either Calgary or Edmonton to bid us farewell. Still, I'm hoping Richard will feel comfortable enough with the group to share some expertise from his past life as a recreation director. He could show us how to make a paper maché buffalo, or lead us in a fingerpainting exercise during one of those long stretches of highway driving.

It all makes me think we should institute some sort of emotional "check-in" at the beginning of each road trip, or even each time folks get back in the van. You know, like you do at the beginning of drama class.

Scene: The Van—First Thing In The Morning

(Everyone tumbles into the van with mugs of coffee.)

Me: Good morning! (*clapping my hands prettily*) I said— good morning!

All: (*mumble-grumble, ad lib "Yeah right" "As if" etc.*)

Me: Settle! Please settle . . .

(Tyler makes a farting noise with his arm pit. Giggling amongst the Gals.)

Me: Very funny, Tyler. Now . . . if everyone could just take their places. Close your eyes . . . (*sternly*) Put it down, Richard. Right . . . now. Before we have a very sticky spill.

Kevin: (*makes a disgusted clicking noise with his tongue*)

Me: Now then . . . time for morning check-in. How is everyone . . . *feeling?*

Kevin: I guess I'm a little worried . . .

Me: (*eagerly*) Yes, Kevin.

Kevin: About sitting in the back seat with Tyler.

Me: I believe we talked about this at last check-in. Intimacy issues may be triggered by our experiences in these unique surroundings. I think we have to be honest with each other. Let's divide into pairs and rap about personal space. Kevin? Tyler? Perhaps you should work together.

Kevin: No! Tyler keeps reading over my shoulder—

Tyler: Kevin stinks!

Kevin: I stink?! Tyler has had altogether too much teriyaki jerky, if you receive my meaning.

(Kevin and Tyler roughhouse in the back of the van.)

Me: Anyone else . . . ?

Norma: (*reading the business section*) Oh look, the dollar's gone up another quarter cent.

Me: Perhaps we can process some of these issues at bed-time check-in. Start the van!

I can't help but think there's a deeper psychological element (a psychosis?) in this group that should be explored and documented. But then I guess if we really worried about people's feelings this trip would never get off the ground.

TEN

WORST FEARS REALIZED

(Crowsnest Pass Part I)

FROM: Patti
TO: The Gals
SUBJECT: Road trip 2003
DATE: April 1, 2003
Hey kidlets! I'm soooooo excited about heading to the scene of one of our province's most infamous crimes. All that plus beef jerky! Who's going to rent the van?

FROM: Me
TO: Patti and the Gals
SUBJECT: Heavenly Transport
DATE: April 2, 2003
The van is secured—we are set! Only 65 more sleeps. Did you know we can actually take a tour into one of the coal mines in that area?

Zowza—our educational component! Checked into B and B scene, there's actually one place that could accommodate all of us.

FROM: Brian
TO: Gals
DATE: May 15, 2003
Sorry for the lapse in communications—I just got back from mounting a truly fabulous Don Giovanni in Austin. The bed and breakfast sounds marvelous. Will there be bacon or is it one of those tiresome continental bread and jam arrangements that I am so often subjected to in the course of my international travels?

FROM: Robert
TO: Gals
SUBJECT: Bacon
Have thoroughly investigated this serious matter. There will be bacon.

FROM: Stephen
TO: Gals
SUBJECT: Re: Bacon and Musicale
Good news about the pork. Very pumped about beef jerky at Longview on the way down. I think we should have a scrapbook. Speaking of educational components, isn't there an interpretive centre at the Frank Slide? I think we should bring musical instruments to play in the van this year. I have a flute and guitar. Is there room for a small keyboard? And of course I'll bring my pitch pipe.

FROM: Kevin and Bob
TO: Gals
SUBJECT: Re: Bacon and Musicale
Suddenly we're almost glad we're not coming this year.

FROM: Brian
TO: Gals
SUBJECT: Saturday Night Follies
You're bringing a keyboard? Surely we could use our combined talents to produce a skit on Saturday night. I don't mind directing

the proceedings. I see us performing a selection of musical numbers from both the classical and contemporary repertoire. Perhaps the writer in our midst could provide a simple scenario.

FROM: Norma
TO: Gals
I'm bringing my tickle trunk! Look, hats for everyone!

FROM: Patti
TO: Gals
I'm imagining lots of snacks. And cozy pajamas. (We can do the skit in pajamas, right?)
Look—Tyler is doing his trick with the banana!

FROM: Richard
TO: Gals
Is it always this much fun?

FROM: Stephen
What a night—every moment truly stage-worthy! (Though we'll never be allowed back at this bed and breakfast, will we?!) Conni's vaude-ville routine was unexpectedly sublime. Oh look, there's bacon and bacon and bacon . . .

FROM: Tyler
Coal mine—scary—there really is a ghost, you can tell. Frank Slide scary too.

FROM: Norma
The guide in the Frank Slide Interpretive Centre isn't nearly as well-informed as I am. I'm taking over the tour, will redesign several of the displays while I'm at it.

FROM: Robert
I drive and drive and drive. I love to drive.

PATTI: Gift shop—souvenirs! Buy many T-shirts and key chains. Spend thirteen hundred dollars.

BRIAN: Mahhhh . . . vell—lous!

RICHARD: Is it always this much . . .

GALS: Arrrrrgggggghhhhhh . . . whooof . . . see you next year . . .

And that's how it happened. So much anticipation, so much dangerous mythologizing, that the trip happened entirely in our imaginations. I contact the group mid-June; they're all surprised to discover that they haven't already been to the Crowsnest Pass.

I reconfirm practical details, warn my colleagues to tamp down unnecessary and inflammatory anticipation, and we actually hit the road this time.

WARNING: This is not a drill! We are going to the Crowsnest Pass.

Serious drama in the Crowsnest Pass.
PHOTO: BOB ERKAMP

ELEVEN
APOCOLYPSE COW

(Crowsnest Pass Part II)

Two rather traumatic things occurred right off the top of this trip, one having to do with food and the other to do with the van.

I've found over the years that these trips have a recognizable pattern in terms of the waxing and waning of our energies. Friday nights always have a frantic edge of hilarity because of the aforementioned anticipation problem but also because we're shedding the worries and anxieties of the previous week so that we can get down to the business of the road trip. We throw back the drinks and talk too loud and stay up too late. Saturday we're bouncing off the walls of the van. Sunday we're bagged, but I like to think of it as a kind of stupefied Zen state. Exhausted, but altered in some sort of essential way.

So. Friday night. Bob and Kevin are unable to join us for the stomp but graciously offer to host the Friday night windup in Calgary. We're to congregate at their beautifully appointed home to tip back a glass of wine or two before going to hang out with Calgary hipsters on 17th Ave. There are snacks and snacks and good red wine and giddy hilarity. We're waiting for a third of our contingent to arrive: Patti has gone to the airport to pick up Stephen and Tyler. We're waiting. We wait some more, eat some more, drink some more red wine.

Patti and the lads finally arrive. There's been an "incident"—Patti scraped the roof rack off the van on her way into the airport parkade! Yeeyikes. I mean at one point or another everybody in this group has been very generous about providing the group with a running gag for years to come. Patti's certainly done her share. Golly, there was the pyrogy pant-ripping incident from Tour 2001. And then the namesake beaver in 2002. Patti just keeps offering up one splendid humiliation after another for our enjoyment. We'll still be giving her a hard time about this in 2020.

At first glance she seems the most unlikely person on the tour to provide this kind of fodder. (Patti is poised and unflappable in all areas of her life.) But maybe this is proof that God only gives you what you can handle. Who better than Patti to shoulder the burden of our ribbing? So after much shouting, hooting, hollering—after holding Patti down on the floor and giving her the bumps and then tickling her until she cries—we get on with our evening.

We stuff our faces with high-quality snacks then make our way to the restaurant. Here it is discovered that the house specialty is beef. Quite by accident, a number of us end up trying the special steak tartar as an appetizer followed by a main course steak. Beef and beef—nothing short of obscene.

I would like to declare a moratorium on talking about food in connection with this road trip. I really would. Please don't think I'm insensitive to the indecency of stuffing our faces when others are not eating very much at all. But I'd be lying if I didn't say that food is pretty much the central focus of these trips. Really though, we Buffalo Gals are deeper than we look. Because the real reason we were choking down the beef that lovely night in June had nothing to do with gluttony and everything to do with social justice.

You see, in May 2003, a single Albertan cow was discovered to have been infected with bovine spongiform encephalopathy. Mad cow disease. It was official—we had a crisis on our hands. The ban on Alberta beef kicked in with brutal speed; borders slammed shut, and the sanctimonious rhetoric began. There was also a blitz of advertising urging support of Alberta ranchers. It worked—Canadians consumed five per cent more beef between 2003 and 2004. If you break down the stat I think you'll discover that most of that five per cent increase occurred on one weekend in June. In southern Alberta. Between Calgary and Blairmore. You see, the Buffalo Gals really felt it was only right to support our ranchers. Besides, how could we miss an opportunity to eat beef and feel morally upright at the same time? So after an extremely festive Friday night, and a sleep disturbed by too much red wine and red meat . . .

Wait. One more thing before we wheel the mangled van out of the parking space and set off down the highway. Something I feel a need to do, now that we have our full complement of Gals.

You see, as we nervously integrated one more person into the group—if even for one more year—I think we all had at least a passing thought about what provided the connective tissue of our little group. We actually came together somewhat haphazardly; I'm not sure it occurred to any of us that we'd be stuck together for years to come.

Perhaps this analysis will yield some insights about why we're together. Moving deep into the backstory . . .

Brian and I were really just children when we met at Red Deer College. He was sitting at a table pretending to be a student advisor; I was decked out in what I considered to be the height of urban fashion. (I have never, ever heard the end of those fateful choices.) We have been the best of friends ever since, the relationship fostered by our creative collaborations and the occasional stint as roommates.

Brian's other particularly close tie in the group is Patti, whom he met while they were both working at the same theatre company in Calgary, years ago. Patti really helps keep Brian in check, partly because of their complementary personalities. Patti is calm, level-headed, and classy; Brian is a merciless tease who can't spend more than about five minutes around someone without giving them some sort of nickname. Usually featuring some thinly-veiled euphemism for a sexual act or body part.

I guess I should feel fortunate that my lifelong moniker is slightly more enigmatic than "dinky-boy" or "puss-pants"; my nickname has a certain tawdry, literary flair. When I met Brian, he was in the midst of reading some Victorian porn featuring a saucy maid called Connie Blunt. Suddenly and forevermore, that was my name. As much as ten years later I would still get the occasional inquiry asking if my real name was a stage name from people who thought my family name was Blunt. (This could only happen in the theatre.)

I have had limited success crazy-gluing a nickname to Brian. "Doctor Faboo" had a short run, although it's exhausting to promote these things with the kind of dogged (and slightly sick) persistence Brian employs to make them stick. Patti has had some success referring to him as "Husky Fit," but even that palls quickly after Brian's been on the Atkins diet for a few weeks. I met Patti through Brian and we now have a friendship distinct from our connection to him.

Patti knows Bob and Kevin partly because they're from the same theatre community, but mostly because Bob and Patti worked together at Alberta Theatre Projects in Calgary. Which is where I met Bob and Kevin, too. Bob scheduled one of my first, big, breakout professional experiences, produced in the new play festival he curated for the theatre. Said play was directed by Stephen. Kevin composed the score for the play I had produced at the festival in 2005.

Norma has worked as an arts administrator extensively in both the Edmonton and Calgary communities, so she has worked with Bob in Calgary, and with Stephen in Edmonton. Stephen and Norma took a theatre history course together at the University of Alberta in the seventies, so they go way back. It wouldn't be too many years later that I admired Stephen from afar in the same department. He was doing a master's in directing, and I was just fresh in from Red Deer College to continue my arts degree.

In the next few years Stephen and I formed a cosmic, creative connection. I was the playwright-in-residence at Theatre Network (where he was the artistic director) for several years, which has provided us with terrific material ever since. (Who could forget the fallout from the dyslexic receptionist? The smelly little garage that served as an office behind the old Jehovah's Witness Hall that served as a theatre?) Stephen has directed several of my premieres, and our working relationships have almost always involved food and drink: litres of coffee and pounds of pound cake, bottles upon bottles of red wine . . .

In later years, before Stephen took a job teaching theatre at the University of British Columbia, we even gathered at his home and canned beet pickles together as the focus for our creative discussions. And we are the past masters, the true originals, the groundbreakers when it comes to the "Liquor! You liquor—you brought her" sub-genre of erudite humour.

Stephen has worked with Bob at Bob's theatre in Calgary, and with Brian on an opera in Vancouver. Norma and Tyler have collaborated on producing literary events.

Maybe I've just described our version of the infamous Canadian theatre "cluster fuck." (A term coined in the eighties to describe the somewhat incestuous nature of the community.) And certainly, just speaking for myself, some of my happiest moments in these friendships have been whilst working together. Seeing someone you really adore in an extremity of emotion or striving can be some of the most high-quality relationship content you'll ever experience.

But hang on, it's not all about work either. Sometimes it's about shared geography or sense of place.

Richard and I have never worked on a theatre project together—he actually works for a folk music festival—but I certainly have a strong connection to his family. My oldest sister babysat his youngest brother. His dad was my junior high principal and even gave me the strap. More than once. Years later Richard and I ended up living next door to one another in the "Moral Imperative Housing Co-operative," wrangling over lawn-mowing, walk-shovelling, and the care and feeding of compost worms. (Richard's a dab hand with the nicknames, too. My co-op monikers ranged from "Environmental Pig" to "Princess") What better preparation for going on a road trip together?

And sometimes it's about love. As a partner in one of the three couples in the van, I think we could leave the origins of my love match, along with those of all these other romantic relationships, for some other book. But while there may not have been obvious affinity between Robert and most of these people, as he is the only one of us not employed in the arts, I think some interesting new connections have formed. Robert and Richard share a love of expensive tequila; Robert and Brian, a love of German humour on the Net. (Long story.) Robert is also Brian's go-to guy for anything connected to computers. And I LOVE THIS: Brian, who is still afraid to download a file from his email—and who knows? maybe he's the smart one—makes ME look like a COMPUTER GENIUS. HAAAAAAAAAAAAAA!

Love—partners—it does raise another question. Norma and Patti have both chosen to shield their husbands from the hurly-burly of the van, the fascinatingly intense dynamics of the Buffalo Gals. Hmmmm . . .

What else? Everyone in the group likes to eat, some more than others. That may be the only thing we all have in common, and even so, there's some variation on that theme. We've established that many of the people in the van work in the theatre. Perhaps that dictates some of the taste in . . . entertainment? Gossip? Actually, if you break down the relationships in the group a little differently, we're sort of equally divided between artists and the folks who support those same artists.

I would argue that there are probably very few jobs as thankless and gruelling as being an arts administrator (with the possible exceptions of teaching junior high, waiting on tables, or freedom fighting). Year after year you're required to prove that you are really and truly reinventing the wheel. Perhaps the most difficult pressure on the job comes from your closest associate, the artistic director. Share my burning vision! Raise money to support my burning vision!

In our little gang we have a nearly equal number of artists and administrators. (I'm counting Robert as the latter because he supports *my* artistic vision.) I can already hear the howls of disagreement and dismay coming from the van; three of the "artistes" are also the heads of their organizations. Drowning in paperwork! Besieged by meetings! But still, first and foremost, these guys are there to do the creative work. The end.

Still, I don't know how any of this helps me define what really brings this group together—and keeps us together—year after year.

The mix of astrological signs in the van is a heady stew of water and earth (mud?), but provides no clues about our raison d'etre. We do have four Libras on the trip. These guys are notorious fence-sitters; their dithering could completely constipate our decision-making process, if we let it. Luckily there's a couple of nasty Scorpios in the group to expedite the process.

There are friendships, sure, but not everyone in the group is bosom buddies with everyone else. It isn't entirely work-related; it isn't even like one big happy family. Some of us really only come together for this event. Are there any clues in appearance or ancestry? I might be tempted to run a blondes-have-more-fun theory up the flagpole, but it's so difficult to tell whether or not our fair-haired friends actually have any blonde hair left.

But I'm just realizing this is confusing to you, gentle reader, since you don't even know what we look like.

Rather than attempting to describe the most obvious charms of my companions, perhaps the most diplomatic ploy is to envision us all in our most idealized state. Surely you've played this game—in the movie of your life, what Hollywood star would play you?

I polled the Gals and received the following suggestions regarding casting.

Brian: Daniel Craig

Kevin: Jake Gyllenhaal

Bob: Richard Gere

Norma: Susan Sarandon

Patti: Lucy Liu

Robert: had no opinions about his star-casting—I chose Russell Crowe, in a bearded phase, on his behalf.

Stephen: Jeffrey Buttle (a figure skater)

Richard: Cate Blanchett playing Daniel Craig

Tyler: Ewan McGregor

Conni: I actually chose Ellen Barkin, but the group was very insistent I be played by Kate Hudson. Who am I to argue with their good taste and judgement?

There. If you met us you'd see that this casting is totally . . . apt. Though I wonder what kind of movie would feature this group of actors? I must confess it makes me think about one of those disaster movies with a big, star-studded cast. The Buffalo Gals version of the Poseidon Adventure? You know, lots of screaming and lots of Shelley Winters and lots of . . .

I think I'd better stop poking this bear with a stick and get on with the tour.

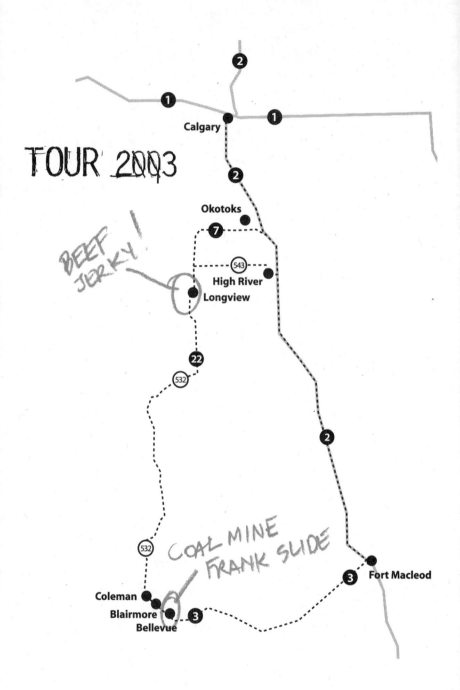

TOUR 2003

BEEF JERKY!

COAL MINE
FRANK SLIDE

The rabble in the rubble at Frank Slide.
PHOTO: PATTI PON

TWELVE
ON THE EDGE OF DESTRUCTION

(Crowsnest Pass Part III)

PRESENT:
Conni, Robert, Brian, Richard, Stephen, Tyler, Patti, Norma
ABSENT:
Bob, Kevin.

TOUR MOTTO: GET IN, GET OUT, GET HUGE!

So. As I was saying . . . Friday night we dine and dine and dine in Calgary, spending about a quarter as much—in total—as it would cost us to fix the van since the roof rack debacle was subsequently ruled to be an inadmissible claim. (I am going to write a whole other book about the f@#king useless nature of vehicle insurance, I swear. Apparently there's a big problem with people willfully ripping the roof racks off their rental vehicles, so the insurance companies had to disallow that as an expense. Darn that Patti and her taste for vandalism.)

Saturday morning: Proceeding southwest from Calgary, we drop in on Okotoks, and return to High River. This is where we made a flying stop in 2000, opting for John Paul's restaurant recommendation rather than a leisurely stroll to view the town's famous murals.

Speaking of John Paul, there's a rumour he's doing his own road trip this year, with a couple of friends from Calgary. It's bound to be a thousand times more posh than anything we do, although it could be tricky to find John Paul's favourite Camembert at the IGA grocery store in Rocky Mountain House. We have a very good time imagining the "other" road trip. I think we half-expect to encounter a Lincoln Navigator on some back road, containing John Paul and some well-heeled compatriots sipping Chardonnay and watching Barry Lyndon on their built-in DVD player.

Anyhow . . . High River is a lovely, not-so-little town of about ten thousand souls at the junction of Highways 2 and 23, alongside the Highwood River. Claims to fame include being the birthplace of former Prime Minister Joe Clark, and a series of murals painted on walls all around town, commemorating various historical events. The Buffalo Gals make history in High River too, by spilling a zillion dollars worth of expensive coffee beans on Main Street. (Although Stephen no longer lives in Edmonton, he does love his Java Jive coffee beans—a year's supply was in the back of the van at the time of the incident.) We scoop up coffee beans for a long while, attracting the attention of curious and incredulous locals. We buy a hat for Norma and then have lunch, as it would probably be at least an hour before we hit Longview beef jerky. (Lord knows no one in this crew needs any more beef—we're only doing this to support the ranchers. I swear.)

It should be noted that this is also the year of the very first scrapbook, purchased in the Saan store in High River. (Some clever clog also thought to bring felt pens and glue sticks.) I really do not feel this report would be complete without including some of the searing insights therein.

Day One of Patti's Control Trip (Journal Entry by Richard)

We met at 9-10-11 for an early escape. A scant three hours later we find ourselves 40 minutes out of town and lost on the highway that goes east and west (not south). Conni says the combination of the "All-Beef Atkins" diet and the Ice Cream from High River is producing less than comfortable results.

Tyler wants us all to buy bras.

2:53 PM (Journal Entry by Stephen)

Here we are, desperate, trying to find the road to Longview. I feel my blood jerky level @ an all-time low and if I don't get some Longview Original into my bloodstream, I may black out! Oh good, we found 418th Avenue and seem to be headed in a good direction. In High River, we met a lady who seemed to be the local welcoming committee. She wanted to know why we were gathering up spilled French coffee beans from the road. (Robert had an angry moment with the Java Jive and hurled it to the ground in a fit of pique.) The lady directed us to the home that Joe Clark was born in.

Longview, Longview, everything will be fine when we get to Longview . . .

Journal Entry by ?

It's the turnoff for Longview—thank God! Otherwise there would have been a revolt. 33 kilometres to beef jerky. It's 3:05 PM—maybe we will get to Crowsnest tonight.

Journal Entry by ?

The sun is starting to sit a little lower in the big sky, and more bugs have blotted the windshield. Longview is coming into sight . . .

Richard:

Hour seven . . . Constance has started offering fashion makeovers to the trapped and terrified van inhabitants . . . is there any escape from this Möbius strip road trip? We just turned the van in a new direction. Much excitement and new hope! In an effort to calm our nerves Conni is relating stories of her favourite accident sightings.

Journal Entry by ?

We have jerked our beef and now resume the journey to what lies beyond High River.

Don't have a cow—just eat it!

When I was a child, cows jumped over the moon. Now . . .

As you may have gathered from these entries, we were lost for a time after leaving Calgary. Interesting . . . we have maps aplenty, and a couple of folks in the van who have lived in and around Calgary for much of their lives. Overall, I'd say this is a collection of very fine minds. No, really—all of the Gals are tolerably intelligent; many of them are dead bloody brilliant. If you laid out all the IQs in the van end to end . . . oh never mind. Yet this isn't the first we've been lost and it certainly won't be the last. How does this happen?

I have a theory. Taken individually, we're all reasonable smarty-pants. Taken together—(and take us together, please!)—we develop a kind of group-think, a collective consciousness that is somewhat addled. You may have seen that great Canadian documentary about corporate culture, *The Corporation*, wherein the filmmaker ascribes a personality (money-grubbing, sociopathic) to a corporate entity. Applying the same logic to our merry little gang, I'd say the personality of our entity is patient, affable, dunderheaded. Oh well . . .

I suppose the big news from Longview is that they have T-shirts. We buy pretty much everything they have in stock, even though they're fairly hideous. (Beige or grey with a big shit-brown cow head on the front.) Still, it suits our purposes: retail therapy and the creation of the new tradition of team uniforms. (Years later we have so much of this wearable art that any one of us could go for a week without donning civvies.)

Just south of Longview we happen upon what I consider to be one of our all-time highlights: Forestry Trunk Road, Highway 532.

(Highway in this case meaning unpaved donkey trail.) Whoever was riding shotgun at that point in the trip, and thus responsible for reading the map, should get full credit for this suggestion. The interlude is not without drama—there's a sign right at the beginning of the route advising us against using the road. (So we know there's some possibility that we'll have to turn back.) Turns out Highway 532 is beautiful but extremely curvy. I think the rare silence that descends during the most treacherous leg of the trip is a sweetly introspective moment. Turns out the folks at the back of the van are actually on the verge of projectile vomit. Just in time . . .

We come around a bend to discover a large hill (small mountain?). We haul the van off to the side of the road. Most of us scramble up the hill, carefully stepping around the stunning alpine flowers which huddle tenaciously in little clusters close to the ground. The view in every direction is heart-stirring. We're skirting Bob Creek Wildland Provincial Park; off to the west are the Rocky Mountains.

This billy goat scramble is also a much-needed break from the hooting, jabbering, and playful bickering in the van. We get some space—from each other and ourselves—hiking up the little mountain. (Norma goes furthest afield to take photos.) It's one of those moments—stretched into an hour—of pure bliss. If nothing else happens for the rest of the weekend, I'll be content to have had this experience.

But of course there's much more fun to come. Highway 532 mutates into something else and dumps us out at Blairmore. We check in at our bed and breakfast. Our hostess, Goldie, is a little bewildered that the Gals aren't actually gals, but she recovers quickly.

The Crowsnest Pass area, snugged up against the BC border, contains several points of interest to the Gals: Coleman, Blairmore, Bellevue, and Frank. During the first half of the last century these little towns serviced a booming business in coal and coke production. Blairmore was also perfectly situated for running rum through the mountains and/or across the border into the US Blairmore's notorious rum-running mayor, Emilio Picariello ("Emperor Pic") was ultimately sentenced to hang after an Alberta Provincial Police officer was shot and killed following a high-speed chase involving Picariello's son.

And there are plenty more surprises in the area's history. As in other mining towns (like Coleman and Drumheller), the unions had a definite impact on the political tenor of their communites. In 1933, the mayoralty and all the seats on Blairmore's town council and school board were won by Communists. (!) That same year, the town council endorsed a petition calling for the abolition of the RCMP. In 1935 they declared a public holiday for the visit of Tim Buck, then leader of Canada's Communist Party. It gets better. In 1934 the Blairmore school board declared a holiday for November 7, the anniversary of the Russian revolution—but not for the marriage of the British Prince George, the Duke of Kent. Much to the unmitigated horror of the town's business people, "Little Moscow" returned "red" slates to office for more than a decade afterwards.

Wow—who knew? Well, some Blairmore folks are surely acquainted with these incidents, but they ain't exactly shouting it from the rooftops. In fact, we couldn't find a single reference to this fascinating chapter in the town's history. Perhaps it's just too mind-boggling for anyone to contemplate. After all, the capital city of this province is routinely referred to as "Redmonton," because we don't robotically return every single seat to the Tories each election. (Just most of them.) In other words, we're a heartbeat away from declaring private property illegal and closing the banks. To the barricades! Sigh . . .

Actually we weren't even thinking about politics when we declared this year's theme "On the Edge of Destruction." The Crowsnest Pass has a history of tragedy and disaster, both man-made and natural. On April 29, 1903, the little town of Frank (east of Blairmore) was devastated by the largest landslide in North American history as nearby Turtle Mountain collapsed. At least seventy-six people were buried alive under tons of limestone. In 1910 a fatal explosion at the Bellevue Mine claimed thirty-one lives. Hillcrest, a little further east, was the sight of the worst mining disaster in Canadian history on June 18, 1914; one hundred and eighty-nine men died. The residents of this area endured three devastating tragedies in just over ten years, then barely had time to catch their breath before World War I started.

It doesn't take long before we've integrated the ripping of the van's roof rack into the Crowsnest Pass disaster narrative. But even that isn't enough for the bloodthirsty Gals—we opt to see some disaster on the big screen as well. Blairmore has a lovely little cinema called the Orpheum, right on Main Street, and this particular night it's featuring Keanu Reeves in *Matrix Reloaded.* The theatre is so darn charming that the film showing may be rather beside the point. There's a balcony above the main auditorium that is furnished like a cozy living room, with easy chairs and couches. If you're a special friend of the owner you can watch the movie from up there, often in the company of her dog. The dog loves his special vantage point, and is mostly well-behaved unless another dog appears on the big screen. (Then you're likely to have your viewing pleasure interrupted by frantic barking.) The credits roll and we're all a bit stunned until we figure out what's just happened. There are no trailers; the movie just starts. How glorious!

The movie is, in my opinion, a dumb-ass gong show of special effects and mind-numbing carnage. I don't mind the bloodbath so much—it is on point with our theme after all—as the careless disregard for any kind of logic in the storytelling. Anyway, the real drama takes place in the auditorium, right next to me. Richard and I are sharing a container of popcorn when suddenly he catapults out of his seat. And runs out of the theatre. It's significant that every single one of the Gals, including me, just thought Richard was deliberately creating a scene. (We're not insensitive, we're just used to theatrics.) We bookmark the dramatic exit for later discussion and continue watching the movie. Richard, meanwhile, is in the lobby getting help from our host: ice cubes to apply to the wasp sting on his left nipple!

After the movie, we have dinner at Pick's Roadhouse, named after the rum-running mayor. Everything about the experience is unremarkable except for the presence of one of the most persistently obnoxious characters we've ever encountered on our trips: the "Buffalo Gals" troubadour, the drunken lounge singer—pain-in-the-ass Andy.

To be fair, we do banter with Andy a little after we've placed our drink order, and once he has a musical cue (the name of our group), he is unstoppable. No, really. Andy will not stop singing "Buffalo Gal, won't you come out tonight?" He circles around us playing his guitar, pops up from behind booths, even sits down at our table for a time. He is particularly insistent that Brian will enjoy his performance, perhaps because Brian is the most unresponsive of everyone. Finally Brian drops to the floor and rolls around in feigned agony, complete with moaning and groaning, imploring Andy to "Please, please stop!"

Andy thinks this is hilarious. He keeps right on singing.

Years later, we still have fond memories of the breakfast Goldie served to us on Sunday morning. There was bacon aplenty and French toast, stuffed with cream cheese and peach preserves. It was a good day to have hot breakfast sticking to your ribs, as the rest of our time in the area would be devoted to viewing scenes of carnage.

Bellevue Underground Mine—Experience the Past!
Put on a miner's helmet and lamp to follow the level and wide corridor taken by coal miners as they worked this mine from 1903 to 1961. Walk along the 300 metres of the old West Canadian Collieries mine tunnel. You will see a "room," a coal chute and original mine artifacts while our guide explains mining techniques.

The mine temperature is 3–7 degrees C so please wear warm clothing and sturdy footwear.

Admission charged, group rates available.

Visit our new gift shop with easy-on-the-pocket souvenirs.
—*Bellevue Mine Tour*

We take the tour and marvel at the hundreds of men—and boys—who toiled away here in order to make their daily bread. (One little trip into this dank, creepy passage is enough for us.) Our tour guide,

Wendy, tells us about a ghost that apparently turns up in photos taken at the entrance to the mine. I'm not surprised that all that human misery has taken some sort of otherworldly form.

Sometime during the early afternoon there's a little sprinkle of rain, so we're just as happy to wander around an interpretive centre reading about the Frank Slide. This catastrophic event is almost more appalling than the mining disaster, if that's possible. While the miner's shift would always be shadowed by the particular dangers of that workplace, the good folks of Frank were mostly snug in their beds when the mountain tumbled down on their heads.

Some of the Gals pore over the geological explanation for the incident, I couldn't care less about the science. (Besides, the Natives in the area practically predicted the slide; they avoided the area around Frank, referring to Turtle Mountain as "the mountain that walked.") The human stories documented in the interpretative centre are the most fascinating; the role of luck and coincidence in life generally— and in this drama—is reinforced over and over. A declined invitation, a botched reservation, a whim to stay the night in a boarding house instead of returning home; all these small decisions meant the difference between life and death.

A watery sunshine warms our backs as we wander through a field of the giant granite boulders that thundered down the side of the mountain and buried the little town. It's by far the most striking graveyard I've ever visited.

It's also, as this group is quick to note, the perfect setting for a) a high fashion shoot, or b) a rock video, or c) a low-budget science fiction film. We riff on various versions of all three as we pick our way through the terrain.

The bill-settling and highly unnecessary last supper take place at Yanni's Salt and Pepper Restaurant in Okotoks. They put us in a back room all by ourselves with a giant bug zapper right by our table. But the waitress has great shoes so all is forgiven by those in the group who care about great shoes. Which is almost everyone.

We've had great shoes, great food, incredible scenery, and a large, fascinating dose of Alberta history. We have had a splendid time with a guest Gal, a temporary Buffalo—Richard. (I don't say it out loud yet, but now that Richard's been with us once, I can't imagine him not being with us forever.) But the agreement was that he would come for one year, and one year only. So I guess we'll cross that bridge when we come to it . . .

Our first team uniforms.
PHOTO: PATTI PON

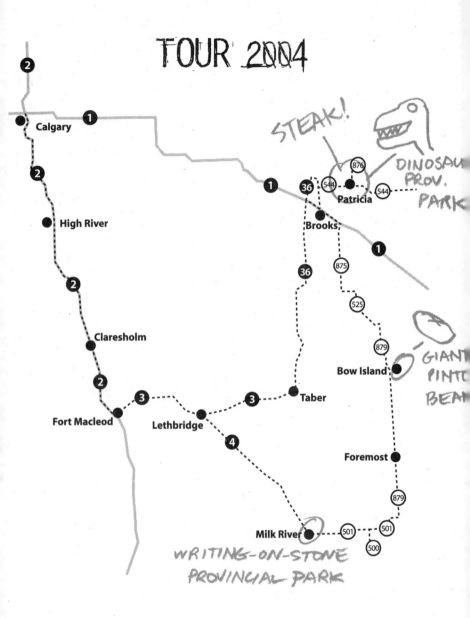

Potato capital of the west.
PHOTO: BOB ERKAMP

THIRTEEN
THE (NEARLY) LOST WEEKEND

PRESENT:

Conni, Robert, Bob, Patti, Norma, Stephen, Tyler, Richard*

ABSENT:

Brian (in Berlin thank you so much), Kevin (missed Friday night)

*(In that splendidly flaccid decision-making style that is so uniquely ours, it's somehow sort of assumed, though never stated outright, that Richard may in fact be joining us again this year.)

Okay, like, some bad shit happened on this trip. Involving food and weather. We just barely survived. And yet . . . you'd never guess any of this by reading the euphoric entries in the scrapbook, reflecting the curious fact that we actually had a marvellous time. There were a couple of moments in the van when we were all laughing so hard that I thought we might endanger ourselves. You know—hyperventilate or faint from the lack of oxygen in that tiny enclosed space.

I think the long hours spent cooped up proved inspirational in

133

other ways, too; this was the year the diarizing and rhapsodizing and poetic riffing in the scrapbook really took off. For this, dear friends, was the year of the haiku—our earthly desires sublimated into verse.

The tour begins with mile-high pie at the Blackfoot Truckstop Restaurant, a famous diner in Calgary, where they really do have the most fantastic, towering slabs of pie. The waitress is right out of central casting (in the tough-talkin' mama category) and the coffee is execrable, all as it should be. Tyler has to be warned to reel it in when he tries to order a "cowpoke breakfast, hold the Levis." (All this, years before *Brokeback Mountain*) The bill has a drawing of a truck on it and a poem (a "pome"?) that finds its way into the scrapbook.

> *Sing While You Drive*
> *45 miles per hour, sing*
> *("Highways are Happy Ways")*
> *55 miles per hour sing*
> *("I'm but a stranger here, heaven is my home")*
> *65 miles per hour sing*
> *("Nearer my God to Thee")*
> *75 miles per hour sing*
> *("When the roll is called up yonder, I'll be there")*
> *85 miles per hour sing*
> *Lord, I'm coming home*
> *PLEASE DON'T DRINK AND DRIVE*
> *Thank you Please Pay Cashier*

Big hunks of pastry and flavoured sugar-goo are dutifully consumed, then we drop off vehicles at Patti's sister's house so that we can all pile into the van.

We're hardly five minutes down the road when it starts . . .

> *A Pie Haiku*
> *My pie is mile high*
> *Mostly air*
> *It's just a teaser*

A haiku is a Japanese poem composed of three unrhymed lines of five, seven, and five syllables, often reflecting on some aspect of nature.

Our haiku um, er, bravely break new ground, setting aside all those stuffy old rules about the number of syllables, and um, the reference to nature. (If we achieved the latter it was entirely accidental.) Okay, I might as well admit it.

The first year we came up with the idea of writing haiku about the haiku-worthy nature we were observing out the window (like cows and pigs and stuff), we thought the scansion was 5/3/5. So we wrote a bunch of terrific little three-line poems, but they weren't actually haiku. Let's call them oh, say "boohoos," or maybe "boo-boos." (Hoodoos? Nope, that was another tour.) Because of recent advances in technology, and the acquisition of various personal communication devices, we now have access to the Internet 24/7. *Now* if we could just verify and/or correct our haiku misinformation. But back in the old days . . . Anyway, the rest of the time on these road trips we've all been really, really smart and literary and intellectual—as you'll see—so maybe we can be forgiven that one little lapse.

The pie is soon a distant memory as we are on our way to Lethbridge, Alberta for our traditional Friday night launch-of-the-tour dinner.

Lethbridge, Alberta's fourth largest city (population: roughly eighty thousand), is about two hours southeast of Calgary. This is dead beautiful country, in my opinion, but perhaps not to everyone's taste. The rolling coulees and endless sky do make for a bit of a moonscape; the wind, worse during the winter months, can drive an inexperienced newcomer to distraction. (No, really—many, many folks go mad in the face of this natural predator.) I love the sense of space; but then, I get stir-crazy in the mountains.

Lethbridge is nestled along the banks of the Old Man River. The High Level Bridge crossing this river is the largest and tallest viaduct in the world, and pretty much the standard postcard view of the city. Peaceful, pretty Lethbridge has a history steeped in conflict. Nearby is the site of the original Fort Whoop-up, at one time hosting a little encampment of lawless American whiskey traders who more or less inspired the formation of the Northwest Mounted Police. (They were charged by the government of the time to straighten out the rowdies and protect the territory.)

Less than a hundred years later, during World War II, hundreds of Japanese Canadians are forcibly relocated from the west coast to the Lethbridge area to work as farm labourers.

Lethbridge's stunning Nikka Yuko Japanese Garden is a testament to the friendship and reconciliation between these two cultures.

I mention a few of the highlights in case you ever find yourself in this neck of the woods. Unfortunately I can provide no guidance, nor share any impressions, because we never went near any of these tourist attractions. Nope. Never went to the Japanese Garden, even though it's the first thing people seem to think of when Lethbridge is mentioned. Never went to the Fort Whoop-up Interpretive Centre, even though nobody knows more about whooping-up than this gang. After hours and hours in a van, already littered with junk food wrappers before we even left Calgary, here we are in Lethbridge, Alberta. And what do we do for entertainment, for enlightenment? What we always bloody well do.

We eat steak.

That said, we do find the most interesting darn steak restaurant possible, and one of the most unique venues for a chow-down we've ever encountered on our travels. The Lethbridge edition of Ric's Grill, a western Canadian chain of high-end steak and seafood restaurants, is located in the city's old water tower. It's a creative use of this classic municipal feature (not quite as iconic as a grain elevator but charming nonetheless) and some of the Gals are just as happy it's not a revolving restaurant. (The same Gals who were suffering from car sickness on the curvy trunk road last year.) An elevator whisks us up to a wraparound view of Lethbridge, some very fine daiquiris, and the obligatory feast.

On the way out of the restaurant we come across another sort of party. A young man wearing a pale blue grad tux (now splattered with vomit) lies sprawled and motionless at the base of the tower. His friends hover, wondering out loud how to get this inert sack of flesh in a motor vehicle. The little scene makes us all feel old. And yet happy that it isn't our grad night. And yet sad for little Josh or Darren or Drew and his pukey tux. And yet delighted we resisted having that third drink. The Germans probably have a word for this. It's not schadenfreude, it's not weltsmertz (world sickness) but maybe it's . . . schadensmertz. Anyway, we step gingerly around the schadensmertz. Grad 2004—you rock.

The entries in the journal about Ric's Grill are predictable . . .

It's alllllllll about the beef! Anonymous

And inscrutable . . .

The date, maybe the first, at Ric's Grill. Will he get his reward at the end of the evening? We hope so. He worked very hard to earn this . . .

I think we might have been speculating about the couple at the next table? And the non-haiku but nevertheless somewhat poetical . . .

Yummy daiquiris at Ric's
The setting sun blasting through the windows
Lena 23 our waitress

Oh Mighty Tower Grill!
Your Jetson's landing pad beckons me
Wish I'd been there . . .

As well as recording impressions of our journey, the scrapbook often reflects on current events. Scrapbook protocol is as follows. On the Saturday morning of the road trip, at our first pit stop for slurpies or coffee, someone buys an armload of magazines and news-papers. These become grist for our scrapbook mill, especially when, as in 2004, one of the names in the news is the same as one of the last names of one of the Gals. This resulted in a stunning col-lage in the scrapbook inspired by the headline: HEATLEY FACES INDICTMENT. The Gals do great scrapbook collages, although there's a tendency for the content to descend quickly and irretriev-ably into bad taste.

The 2004 scrapbook also features a tribute to Marlon Brando, who died just before our trip, and a few rather badly judged "separated at birth" pairings (Paul Martin and Saddam Hussein?) culled from publications ranging from the *National Post* to the *National Enquirer.*

So. After a restful night in the Lethbridge Econo Lodge and Suites, we wander down the street for breakfast. We're joined there by Kevin, who'd had a gig in Calgary the night before and then driven down to meet us in the morning. (This will complicate matters later in the trip.)

The main purpose of dragging our troupe down to this end of the province is to see one of the wonders of the world. Nominated by Parks Canada and the Feds as a World Heritage Site (no word on the outcome yet), Writing-on-Stone Provincial Park contains the greatest concentration of rock art in North America. The Siksika, the Blackfoot Nation which dominated southern Alberta several hundred years ago, named the site along the Milk River "Aisinai'pi—'it has been written.'" What they found (and what they themselves augmented) were hundreds of petroglyphs (rock carvings) and pictographs (rock paintings).

The park is a vast and dramatic setting, characterized by coulees and hoodoos. It also features a North West Mounted Police outpost reconstructed on its original site as well as an abundance of wild creatures. The Writing-on-Stone Provincial Park website provides a listing of the nature one might hope to encounter in this area. Bird species include: prairie falcon, great horned owl, short-eared owl, American kestrel, cliff swallow, and the introduced ring-necked pheasant and grey partridge. Other species roaming the park include mule deer, northern pocket gophers, skunks, raccoons. There are also salamanders, boreal chorus and leopard frogs, plains spadefoot toads, garter snakes, bullsnakes, prairie rattlesnakes . . . and more.

Two things worth noting: the lovely poetry of a list that includes cliff swallow, plains spadefoot, and boreal chorus frogs.

The other thing is that the rattlesnake is not given any particular emphasis. And let me tell you, that in no way reflects reality, since every freaking guide and hotel manager and gas station attendant in this area of the world mentions the rattlesnakes. "Enjoy your trip—

careful not to step on a poisonous snake." Or "Welcome to Milk River—oh by the way, the nearest major hospital is two hours away in Lethbridge. Have a great day!" Perhaps I exaggerate. (Who, me?) Perhaps it only came up once or twice. And maybe a snakebite isn't all that serious when it gets right down to it. Yeeeeeeeyikes!

The Alberta Online Encyclopedia provides a dramatic description of the landscape here.

"At the end of the last ice age, eleven thousand years ago, torrents of water from melting mountain glaciers turned into a raging river slicing through soft sandstone deposited eighty million years earlier on what had been a shallow marine shelf. As the glacial waters ebbed and the Milk River slowly shriveled to the gentle meander it is today, a steep and immense canyon was left, its exposed cliffs, some as high as fifty metres, further eroded by wind, water and the cycle of freezing and thawing. The result: a landscape at once forbidding and compelling. In sunlight, it is a garden of shadows, unearthly, almost unnerving. Even the most dedicated disciple of the rational can't elude the feeling that Writing-on-Stone is a supernaturally charged spot."

Yeah! Like Head-Smashed-In, this place has a mystical feeling that is difficult to understand or describe unless you've been there. It feels a bit like being in an enormous natural dinosaur cathedral. It's more physically imposing than say, the Plains of Abraham, and though the Writing-on-Stone site may not have borne witness to one such significant battle, it still feels resonant with history.

We opt for a guided tour of the site. Having read our brochure, we know that we're advised to wear socks and shoes, as a protection against rattlesnakes. We suit up in the van and join the tour on a little landing by a cliff face. Did I mention how hot it is? It's really, really hot. And maybe I had a little too much breakfast. I'm afraid the time has come for truth-telling, shame-sharing, mea culpa, mea lazy, sensitive princess.

Because I didn't go on the tour. I tried, I really did.

Don't get me wrong, our guide Bonnie is fascinating and funny. But five minutes into her patter I feel beastly, absolutely boiled in a bag. I can't imagine another two hours of this. So I repair to the parking lot while my jeering compatriots continue with the tour. I stretch out on a seat of the van, eat a few M&Ms. I have a vague notion that I'll nap but it is hopelessly stuffy inside this boiling metal crate. So I open the doors, hoping to create a little cross-breeze, praying for a wee shut-eye, a little respite from the constant warbling and wha-hoo-doodling of the other Gals . . .

But suddenly they're back, and looking mighty disgruntled. What happened—why didn't they go on the tour? Why oh why? I sit up and prepare to scooch over so the hoards can pour in, but instead, they surround the van. They look menacing. I call out—"there are still some Gummi bears left, honest!" Tyler giggles malevolently. The others call out random taunts and insults. "Princess!" "Little Miss Muffet!" "Wanker!" Then, on a signal from Stephen, the Gals start to rock the van back and forth until finally it tips over and begins to roll down a steep incline toward the Milk River!

And then of course, I wake up.

Journal Entry by Richard

Went to see the pictographs and such. Very educational and uplifting. Conni turned back after a few minutes—we thought because of heat sensitivity, but in fact it was because she felt inspired to go on her own vision quest. Sure, it wasn't exactly four days in the wilderness without food or water, but no one said two hours in a hot van with warm gummi bears was any picnic either. How disappointing that her spirit guides turned out to be "peanut" and "plain" from the M&M commercials . . .

Clipped from the *National Enquirer*, context God Knows What:

There was a fear that overcame her, linked to a sensation of being slightly out of control, as though her body were not altogether hers or the line between the world out there and her in here was very thin.

Someone else terribly witty drew a graphic representation of my "vision quest" in the scrapbook. This features some very poor artwork, and the words "Hilary McDuff" repeated over and over again. Honestly! You'd think I wasn't considered to be thoughtful, deep, and searingly intelligent!

I've consulted my colleagues for an actual description of the tour. The highlights seemed to be as follows.

1. The Gals saw a rattlesnake!

2. Ponoka—mine and Richard's hometown—gets a mention on the tour as it's actually a Cree word meaning "black elk."

3. Bonnie the tour guide was smart and funny.

4. The Gals saw a rattlesnake!

We do a little tromping around on our own after the tour—I try to be especially lively while climbing a hill that provides a vantage point to view the Milk River winding off into the distance. Beauteous! We're sure we can see half of Montana off to the south. And everywhere there's sky-sky-sky. This would be a fantastic place to come on a canoeing trip. (The Gals in canoes? Maybe not so much. Remember the roof rack.)

And now it's time to pile into the van . . . clouds darken as we proceed north on Highway 879. According to the scrapbook . . .

Fierce eugenics argument erupts in the van—we really need a drink. Conni and Richard defend the Hutterite way.

I'm not entirely sure how Hutterites and eugenics are connected, best not to speculate.

The vision of a frosty glass of draft beer in a small-town tavern begins to loom large in our imaginations. The next town on the route is Foremost.

4:55 PM. Only minutes from Foremost I feel the collective tongue of the van hanging out. Please God—let there be a bar in this oasis!

Curiously, there ain't no bar in Foremost. (And no joy in Mudville.) How is this even possible?! We're out of van snacks and there are those among us who are actually—gaspé—a little peckish. Nothing to do but soldier on, continuing north toward Bow Island.

Bow Island, "bean capital of the west," made it onto our highly-contested, terribly discerning itinerary because of the giant pinto bean we hope to see there. Yup, "Pinto MacBean" is the town's mascot, built to draw attention to the town's dry, edible bean industry. Brian will be very, very sorry he missed this just so he could spend the time in stuffy old Berlin. Those of us who have moved heaven and earth to be on the trip only regret that we're a few weeks too late to see the Bow Island Bean Pot parade.

It's nearly 6 PM when we've finished posing for the required photo grouped around the eighteen-foot tall statue of Pinto MacBean. Everyone's hungry; we plan to reprise the Patricia cook-your-own-steak bar tonight, but that's hours off. We find a rundown little burger joint and we fools rush in . . .

What to order for a little tide-you-over snack? The gluttonous tradition of these road trips more or less demands that one just throw caution to the wind and order a burger. Or the now infamous deep-fried mushroom balls.

Ohhhhhh Nelly on a stick, this food is bad. No, I'd have to say this is the most stomach-churning toxic waste we've ever encountered on the trip. Or anywhere. None of us finish our food. Richard is the only one among us who hasn't ordered anything. Oh wise Richard . . .

There is a teaching moment here, though. Or just a tip. When in doubt, check the state of the bathrooms before you order. That's what Richard did, and the experience completely killed his appetite. This surly reportage isn't meant to disparage the earnest efforts of the proprietors of _____ Drive-In; I only include this account to demonstrate the unquenchable, undeniable good spirits of Gals in the face of adversity. Sure the experience inspired a queasy little collage in the scrapbook, featuring the headline: "Most of us ignore the deadly and common threat of food." But the very next entry . . .

Happy to report that "The Pit" at the Patricia Hotel will be open until 10! We loved Pinto MacBean!

Are we plucky or what? And by now . . . quite peckish. The plan for the evening is to drive like maniacs (on Highway 879, west on Highway 3, then north on Highway 36) to get to the Patricia cook-your-own-steak bar (by 9? 9:30?), then retrace our steps to stay in a B&B south of Brooks. In other words, a heck of a lot of to-ing and fro-ing on the same stretch of highway. Careening around the countryside in our white van, way behind schedule but doggedly determined to return to the scene of our earlier triumph, I wonder what Pat the waitress from the Patricia Hotel Steak Pit would say about our evening's plan. I have a fair idea . . .

Perhaps the sane alternative to this plan would be to eat in some Greek pizza restaurant in Brooks, the likes of which we've seen many times before, at some reasonable dinner hour. Then retire to the bed and breakfast for a pot of tea and some fellowship. Of course if we'd had breakfast earlier, spent less time at Writing-on-Stone, begun the drive north sooner . . . sure, we never would have had the disgusting grub in Bow Island. But where's the fun in that? We all seem to enjoy the experience of doing something completely hare-brained. Going to great lengths to accomplish very little. Moving heaven and earth to enrich a tradition, or create a tradition. It's our philosophy, our noble quest.

And of course, if we'd done the reasonable thing, then we never would have had these gifts to add to the literary canon. The agony and the ecstasy . . .

> *Bow Island repaste*
> *Queasy grease*
> *Don't finish the fries!*

> *Drive-in Restaurant*
> *Urgent Need*
> *Now filled with Regret*

> *Cold steel pressed to flesh*
> *Pit till 10*
> *Patricia Hotel*

> *Patricia rib-eye*
> *Oh sweet cow*
> *Needs no condiments*

> *Conni reveals her true farm roots by mistaking goats for "small horses"—hi-larity ensues!*

Upon sober reflection, I do think that the Gals need to write a policy paper on the wisdom of visiting the same tourist attraction twice. Part of the issue here is that certain members of the group (Richard, Robert) had never been to Patricia and we thus felt honour-bound to provide this opportunity. But personally I find the experience to be a little underwhelming. Sure the beef is great, but Pat, our original purveyor of carnivore bliss and the undisputed sultan of deadpan, is no longer working here. The infamous poster ("Keep your city out of my country!") is gone, replaced by something hopelessly innocuous. The kicker is:

On the wall by the bar, there's a sincerely gushing thank you card from "Mike and Ron, the Bagel-Biting Latte Sippin' Fags from LA."

Now this, in and of itself, is not necessarily proof that rural Albertans are open-minded, liberal—That's SMALL "L" liberal by God, never ever *Liberal*, we gather a bucket fulla spit in our mouths and curse that Frenchie forever and don't pretend you don't know who I mean; a pox on the head of all those Scotch-swigging, NEP-promoting traitorous gits. We'd as soon give votes to the fence posts between your yard and mine as give any of those weasels a seat. The "L word" is something very different in these parts let me tell ya—

Golly, who opened the Texas gate for that rancorous little side-bar? As I was saying, perhaps the postcard by the bar isn't exactly proof that all Albertans are live-and-let-live folks who welcome diversity and difference in all its forms. But we're probably no more or less tolerant than the full range of mullet-sporting yahoos driving pimped-out half-tons in any part of this great land. And we—Albertans—are chock full of surprises. Only not when it comes to electing our governments. As we are enjoying our sixth annual road trip, the Conservatives are enjoying their thirty-third consecutive year in power, the last twelve under King Ralph. Er, um . . . Ralph Klein.

Back into the van. We hit the liquor store in Brooks so we'll have a little something for a night cap. Now that darkness is finally overtaking us at nearly 11 PM, we have a wee bit of trouble finding the Lake Shore Bed and Breakfast. But eventually, and with very little snappishness or whimpering from the back of the van, we arrive.

It's a huge, newish house right on the banks of beautiful man-made Lake Newell. Bob's here under duress. He objects to B&B's on principle, having evidently had some terrible experiences with claustrophobic, Victorian, frou-frou cottages and over-solicitous, tea-toting hosts. But this place seems to meet his exacting standards—it's spacious and comfy, and the owners seem content to leave us alone. We open our red wine and ease into the hot tub that is bubbling away out on the patio.

Sunday we wake up to fog on Lake Newell, obscuring almost everything but a beautiful blue heron posing gracefully for our benefit.

What I had envisioned for this next part of the road trip was that I would host a tour of another of my favourite places in the province, possibly in the entire country: Dinosaur Provincial Park, a Unesco World Heritage Site. Over the last hundred years approximately one hundred and fifty complete dinosaurs have been excavated from this area, as well as countless other dinosaur bones. Most of the material on display at the world-famous Tyrrell Museum in Drumheller is taken from Dead Lodge Canyon, part of Dinosaur Provincial Park.

The approach to the park is reminiscent of Head-Smashed-In. As in: one drives along endlessly, with flat, relatively barren landscape in every direction, thinking you must have misunderstood the directions. Then suddenly you're going down a hill—and the world just falls away. You're on another planet, plunging into a kind of miniature Grand Canyon. A sculptural marvel, a hoodoo theme park—it is truly impressive. You can drive right down into the base of the canyon, and even camp there if you like. There are hiking trails aplenty through the hoodoos, and while it's often beastly hot, one tends to step lively due to the possibility of encountering rattlesnakes, black widow spiders, or scorpions.

None of this is destined to be on the program that day in July. The rain has gone from drizzle to downpour, and the fog that loomed so prettily over Lake Newell this morning is completely obscuring the view of the park. A few muddy-looking hoodoos poke out of the soupy mist, but there's no hint of the astounding vistas that surround us. I can tell my compatriots are underwhelmed. I want to weep with frustration—this is one of the coolest places in the world, honest! We wander the site for a while; might as well, we're here. Buy some coffee at the snack bar, then leave.

We're so desperate for stimulation at this point that we actually spend about half an hour in the Dinosaur Country Store looking at second-hand books and lame souvenirs.

Even this makes me bitter as there used to be a vintage country store just minutes away from here, in Millicent. "Uncle Tom's Cabin" sold work clothes and staples and cheese chipped off a huge block. The owner, Tom Charleton, may have been the only card-carrying Liberal—and certainly the only Trudeau-lover—in southern Alberta. The Canadian flag outside his store was lowered to half-mast on two occasions: when Mahatma Gandhi died in 1948 and, as Tom Charleton was keen to tell you—the day Canada died. (May 22, 1979, when Pierre Elliott Trudeau lost the election to Joe Clark, and the Conservatives came to power.) Alas, Tom is no longer with us. I can't help but wonder what grand gesture he might have made when Stephen Harper came to power . . .

Back at the "Dinosaur Country Store," many of us buy hats with a "Dinosaur Provincial Park" logo. Someone buys several packages of jerky for sharing. We've got a long drive ahead of us. A really long drive. We drive and drive and drive. Through uninspiring countryside shadowed by scowling skies. Some of the Gals resort to writing essays in the scrapbook in order to pass the time. A couple of the entries source the deep vein of grant-writing expertise in this van.

Re/Visioning Alberta—A Proposal from Buffalo Gals

Contemporary Alberta reflects all aspects of global life today. Popular media would see the province as a "redneck backwater," but it is the intent of the Buffalo Gals to represent the real Alberta, the Alberta best appreciated in the grassroots experience.

Buffalo Gals performance techniques will bring a deeper apperception of the concerns of everyday Albertans to the public. These techniques, which include "eating," "drinking," "shopping," and "sleeping," as well as "scrapbooking," "photography," and "oral history-taking," provide a fresh approach to this piece of theatre.

And a slightly more impressionistic approach:

Buffalo Gals: The Documentary
No filming in the van. VAN = SACRED SPACE.
Craft service would feature fresh Alberta products and gummi bears.
We need matching sweat suits.

Not to be outdone in the bafflegab department . . . Richard has a degree in landscape architecture, which he puts to use in his essay.

Buffalo Gals—Pinto MacBean Project
Fighting the current concept of urban cultural homogeneity of place by demonstrating via photography and journal entry how the distinct inclusion of fibreglass icons into the rural landscape has created a resonant unique-ness of place whose transposition to the modern civic landscape would undoubtedly relieve the blight of the "ennui of modernity" that faces modern civic design.

Uhh . . . yeah, right. I think what he's saying is that we could all use a little Pinto MacBean in our lives.

Suddenly we are faced with some harsh realities. We see a sign for "Jenner," which corresponds with a little dot on our map, many kilometres EAST of where we want to be. We've been going the wrong direction for quite some time now. Sigh. It's nothing a U-turn won't fix.

But now we begin the most inane, desperate, confusing, soul-destroying leg of our journey. We must, of course, retrace our steps after this long, eastward detour. Then we have to go all the way back to Lethbridge so that Kevin can pick up his car. (We really, really did not think this one through.) The van is nosed south again and we cheerfully (!) revisit some very familiar territory. My memory of this trip is that we drove up and down Highway 36 about nine times through muddy landscapes we were so sick of we could draw them in our sleep.

Mind numbing highway
No sign seen
We've been here before

But we laugh and laugh and laugh. About . . . ? Don't remember.
I do know that part of what elevates this little interval from inanely
futile to almost productive is that we plan next year's trip, which we
have dubbed:

BUFFALO GALS 2005: THE INTOLERANCE TOUR!

Happily for us, the home of Jim Keegstra (of Holocaust-denying
fame), the former workplace of Jim Keegstra (Eckville High School),
and the home of Aryan Nation Warrior Priest Terry Long are all within
spitting distance of one another. We amuse ourselves with many different versions of next year's itinerary. Really we're just trying to keep
our minds off the fact that we're all getting very, very hungry. Thank
goodness Bob's there to impose order and discipline in the van. (Like
if someone needs to be lashed to the luggage rack for a timeout—and
some fresh air—while we career down some country road, Bob's usually the one to make the call.) And on this fateful day, when some of
the Gals won't stop talking about lunch even though it might be many
hours off, Bob's the one to provide the teaching moment. ("Shut up
about lunch.")

We've pinned our hopes on Vauxhall, Alberta, the "potato capital of
the west" and home of Sammy and Samantha Spud. Also allegedly the
location of a fancy-arse deli restaurant described in an Alberta restaurant guide written by the former restaurant critic from the *Edmonton
Journal.* Problem is, we don't actually have the guide with us. As we
barrel down the highway toward the giant spuds, I'm trying really,
really hard to remember the name of our proposed lunch venue.

Hunger wracks the van
Heart breaking
We drive in circles

On this grey, rainy, Sunday afternoon, they've pretty much rolled up the sidewalks in Vauxhall. There's no sign of any funky little eateries that would rate a mention in the where-to-dine book. We settle on hot sandwiches and gravy at Nonna's Pizzeria. On the bright side, there's gooseberry pie.

We do our bills, take soggy photos in front of Sam and Samantha Spud, then drive all the way back to Lethbridge so Kevin can pick up his car.

From the Scrapbook . . .

Afterthought: How many times in one trip can you pass by "One Tree Road"?

Does that include bacon?
PHOTO: BOB ERKAMP

TOUR 2005

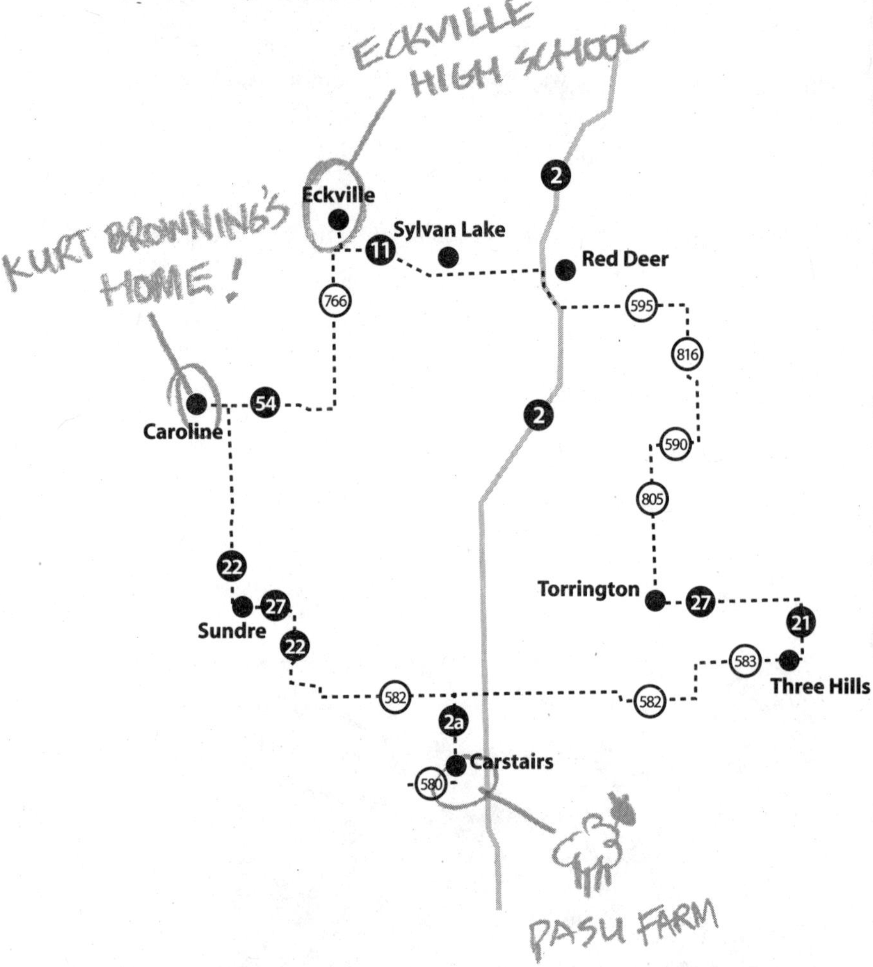

ECKVILLE HIGH SCHOOL

KURT BROWNING'S HOME!

Eckville

Sylvan Lake

Red Deer

11

766

54

Caroline

595

816

590

805

2

2

22

Torrington

27

21

27

Sundre

22

583

Three Hills

582

582

2a

Carstairs

580

PASU FARM

Scene of the infamous international incident.

PHOTO: PATTI PON

FOURTEEN
THE INTOLERANCE TOUR

PRESENT:

Bob (Mr. "I Wanna Pick My Lamb"), Conni ("Gopher Princess"), Norma ("Ropers? You Roper You Brought 'er"), Brian ("CurlyCuts"), Stephen (Mr. "I'm NOT driving this f-ing van all weekend"), Robert (Mr. "I Hope I Get My Skating Pants"), Patti ("Don't Rubber Boots")

ABSENT:

Richard, Kevin

It should be noted that this year's trip could easily have had several other themes or titles. After all, 2005 was the year of Alberta's Centennial. If the group had only been thinking clearly . . . Again, individually we is plumb-diggidy smart. As a group . . . I direct you to earlier remarks about the sweet-natured but dumb-assed Buffalo Gal collective consciousness. Anyway, you'd think one of the geniuses in this group of funding mavens and artistic visionaries would have thought to make a grant application on our behalf.

There was definitely money available—surely we could have scored a couple hundred dollars for the van rental. Surely we could have whomped up some convincing bafflegab about producing the Buffalo Gals Alberta Centennial Scrapbook. We could have called the tour "Alberta 100: A Century of Road Trips" or "Alberta Rocks—On and On and On." If someone in the group had really been on their game we could have scored a big grant and chartered a plane to fly to all the best road trip locations in the province. We could have published the scrapbook AND produced the documentary. But no one thought to belly up to the public trough. Go figure.

Or perhaps alternative sources of funding could have been found, like sponsorship. We could have had "The Epcor Alberta 100 Road Trip." Or "PetroCanada Centennial Tour." I'm not sure yet how this would have influenced our itinerary except that we'd probably be wearing hard hats in most of the photos.

But in truth, this is probably something Brian and I should take responsibility for. After all, we were the only ones in the group engaged in an Alberta Centennial project in 2005. I was hired to write a kind of variety show planned for the Queen's visit to Edmonton; Brian worked as an assistant director on the project. It's one of the oddest gigs I've ever been involved with: fantastic colleagues and disastrous outcome.

The show was slated for performance in the Commonwealth Stadium—outside—on the May long weekend. Are you seeing the humour in this already, or do you need a few more clues? Alberta? Weather? Thousands of hapless citizens heading for natural parks for their first camping trip of the season, all set to huddle in rain-soaked sleeping bags? Or, in the case of the Alberta Centennial Show, to line up to get into Commonwealth Stadium to see the Queen. Well, much to my great disappointment the whole event was foreshortened due to freezing temperatures and rain. A dancer slipped and fell on the stage during the first half hour of the performance. My part of the show, featuring Alberta musicians and a couple of gorgeous narrators (Lorne Cardinal and Paul Gross), was cancelled and replaced by the performers huddling together under the band shell to sing "Four Strong Winds" with Ian Tyson. And that, my dears, was that.

I was really, really sick about this, especially since it could have so easily been avoided. The director had a rainout plan, but it was cut from the budget by the powers-that-be. In Calgary they performed their whole Queen show from start to finish—in a covered venue. In Edmonton we made Her Royal Highness drag some stylish furs out of her trunk in order to do a chilly walkabout to accept bouquets from shivering children dressed in ethnic costumes, and to wave regally to a half-filled stadium of hardy souls sitting on hot water bottles. Cripes! Darn it all! Tarnation! Honestly, I was probably the only person there who was upset about going home early; since everyone else came to see the Queen and she came through in style.

If I was a little bit more dogged (or dog in the manger) than I am, I might have made the Buffalo Gals act out my Queen Skit in the van. Don't think it didn't cross my mind. Instead I opted for making them all listen to my long-winded (but gripping) account of the day's tragic events. I'm sure I saw Stephen nodding off during the good parts. And every single one of the Gals failed the quiz afterwards.

This is all by way of saying we could easily have had a Centennial-themed road trip in 2005. Or . . . we could have called the trip "On the Edge of Destruction—Part II." The torrential rains and resulting floods in central Alberta that weekend were truly apocalyptic. But then maybe that was sort of appropriate given the theme of the trip.

A joke made in the van between Vauxhall and Taber in June, 2004 about "The Intolerance Tour" had taken shape as a real road trip idea . . .

James Keegstra, an auto mechanic, former mayor, and former high school teacher in Eckville, catapulted to world attention in 1984 when he was stripped of his teaching certificate and charged under the Criminal Code of Canada with "willfully promoting hatred against an identifiable group." Turns out Keegstra had tossed out the high school social studies curriculum in favour of teaching from his own private library.

Keegstra taught his students that the Holocaust was a myth cooked up by the "treacherous," "barbaric," "money-loving" Jews in order to garner sympathy. Students who parroted Keegstra's views generally got higher grades than those who didn't. (Duh!) Keegstra took his case to the Supreme Court and lost by a narrow margin, making headlines around the globe and solidifying Alberta's reputation as a redneck, racist, rathole of anti-Semitism and dangerous lunacy. And if there was ever any danger of that notion dying down . . .

Terry Long, "High Aryan Warrior Priest" of the Aryan Nations, lives right up the road in Caroline, Alberta. There seems to have been a real maelstrom of activity amongst the Aryan Nation/Heritage Front folks in the early nineties. (Long set up his infamous "hate line" dial-a-racist-rant in 1991.) But Long was still in the news as late as 2004, with an announcement that he was setting up a "white power" training camp in Caroline.

Golly—that's downright scary. And of course, darkly irresistible to a vanload of artists, homosexuals, Jews, and folks who believe that not only did the Holocaust occur, but it was actually a very bad thing. We decide to visit both Caroline and Eckville. We have nothing in particular in mind once we get to these locales. No confrontations, or placards, or social activism, or guerilla theatre skits. Maybe we just want to go and see if we pick up some kind of vibe. On a much lighter note, Caroline is also the hometown of international figure-skating superstar Kurt Browning. We're hoping there'll be a museum. And T-SHIRTS! And then there's the red meat component of our trip to consider. The Saturday night feast . . .

As I mentioned earlier, Stephen has been whining about the PaSu sheep farm ever since that very first time we drove down Highway 2 and he saw the sign. We should have given in earlier, but we had visions of wool-carding demonstrations and sheep-shearing contests. When it looked like we would be going right by the PaSu sheep farm—again— and that they might be able to feed us, we finally relented. Stephen was ecstatic—as far as he was concerned we could have called the trip "Yahoo PaSu."

You may be asking yourself what sheep farming has to do with intolerance. Possibly nothing. Unless we say we'll be demonstrating our own intolerance of lambs or vegetarians or . . . oh hell, these road trip themes are merely loose organizational principles. Nothing more.

Ever since the glorious Japanese–Mormon hunting lodge of 2000 we've tried to locate the most unique accommodation in the area. After a little preliminary search on the Internet I thought I'd really scored. I found a place where we could all sleep together in a teepee! Or in a cowboy bunkhouse!

From: Bob

Date: May 22/05

Is this too lamb-centric a theme? What about all the other fine live-stock in our province? Should we not be saluting them as well in this our centennial year? We should at least have some pork in honour of the premier.

En tout cas: all fine by me. Is there no hoedown in Red Deer Friday night? Be nice to eat somewhere besides Glen's, as fascinating as the teapot shop is. Too bad that production of Edward Albee's "The Goat" isn't still running. Look, another animal!

I can't seem to link to the B and B. The bunkhouse terrifies me: I just know I'll be sitting out all night stoking the fire and making sure the cowboy coffee stays hot. The howl of the coyotes in the distance, etc.

Hot tip: the Kurt Browning Museum in Caroline comes highly recommended. Skaters!

Definitely Three Hills pie. I bet they have a great turkey entrée. Another barnyard animal—yippee!

And I'm fine with the rack in PaSu.

Bob

As you can see, response from the Gals to the teepee idea was somewhat mixed. But then it turned out the whole place was booked for a wedding, so we were saved from negotiating these all-too-intimate sleeping arrangements.

Friday, June 17, 2005

We meet in Red Deer at the cutest little martini bar you've ever seen: The Velvet Olive. It's a bit of work to find the place, tucked into a back alley right in the middle of downtown. It's raining out and some of our number are dangerously hungry and damp; others are skeptical about the bar's existence. So it's all the sweeter when we finally belly up for a perfect cocktail. This is followed by dinner at the Rusty Pelican, a festival of fine wine, succulent beef, and mouth-watering desserts. Delicious. By the time we retire to the Comfort Inn we are well and truly stuffed.

The next morning gets off to a rollicking start. HAAAAAAA.

After bacon and eggs and, for some, a "sausage sampler" at Denny's we attempt to peruse the wares at the Red Deer farmer's market. I'm not just sure what we had in mind since we'd already had breakfast. (Maybe we were attempting to have some vaguely nutritious road snacks?) We do manage to locate the farmer's market, but they're not really open for business yet.

It's drizzling rain, a grey and uggy start to our trip. But we still have one stop before we hit the open road. We decide we really cannot leave Red Deer until we get down on one knee in front of Francis the Pig. We gather around our brave piggy pal for a photo op just as the heavens open up for a good old, slam-down, torrential-type rain. We're distraught, lost . . . until someone spots a retail opportunity across the street. And the sign we Gals can never resist: Sale-sale-sale!

Wei's Western Wear will perhaps never be the same. The Gals fan out and get serious immediately after entering the store. Norma's trying on boots. Several of the lads are bunched up in the jacket section. Patti and I wrestle over some beautiful, linen, cowboy dress shirts. A coupla hundred dollars later, we brave the outdoors again, blow kisses at Francis, and head southeast to revisit another old Buffalo favourite: the Torrington Gopher Museum.

Around about this time, Tyler announces that he has left his leather jacket at the Denny's. Tyler has, more than once, employed this rather creative strategy for making us return to a location he particularly liked. It's the old "I think I forgot my leather jacket somewhere" gambit, and it works every time. Well it works with most of us anyway. In the instance of the jacket, I think Bob just said, "Someone's probably stolen it by now anyway." (Is this tough love translated into road trip terms? Like . . . "You do not have to pee. Sit on your foot. Think of Regina.") The rest of us are gullible sorts and have always agreed to double back to pick up Tyler's wallets and coats and gummi bears.

I find I really must pause here to note that there seems to be quite a lot of airtime in the scrapbook devoted to the idea of "cheerleader topping" on a pizza. Presumably this is something that came up Friday night . . . ? Did someone find this on the menu at Denny's? Impossible to say. I've checked with my colleagues and none of them remember either, but it seems to have been the source of some hilarity that first day.

> *Foul pizza topping*
> *Cheerleaders*
> *Intolerance tour*

Or . . .

Day one and the search begins for sustenance and the elusive gourmet black gold with a little cow juice on the side . . . but no cheerleader topping please.

The scrapbooks are full of these inscrutable references to experiences that obviously seemed very, very funny at the time. But obviously not funny enough to be burned into anyone's cerebral cortex.

Off to Torrington to check in on our beloved rodents. All is exactly as it should be, with the brilliant addition of "The Torrington Gopher Call Song," which the gopher museum host eagerly offers to play—insists on playing—for us.

The lyrics, penned by Dennis Oster, are sung to the tune of "The Wabash Cannonball."

> *The Torrington Gopher Call Song*
> *Listen to the whistle, O hear the gopher call,*
> *As they roam from early springtime*
> *To the late part of the fall.*
> *They dig their holes with pleasure,*
> *Five for every one.*

Front door, back door, side door
And two dug just for fun.
There's millions of these rodents
That are causing such a fuss,
They dig their home in the prairie loam
Turning everything to dust.
If you fret and worry that the gopher will be gone
You can always take some with you
And release them in your lawn.
The moral of this story is to be wise
Before you speak
Lots of us do like them
But their damage is not cheap.
There always will be gophers
Their lives not in hand,
So just sit back and watch them as they
Dig up all our land.

Now that I've looked at the lyrics more closely, I realize that this is Torrington's response to criticism from around the globe. (More evidence of outrage has piled up in the bulging scrapbook by the guest book.) I think I understand why the song plays in a constant loop during our entire visit—we're the victims of a brainwashing experiment. We could have told the kindly volunteer that we were "friendlies" and saved her the trouble of drilling the lyrics into our heads.

The big news is—and this falls under the heading of retail opportunities—the big news is there are finally TORRINGTON GOPHER HOLE MUSEUM T-SHIRTS!!! We all buy at least one, overjoyed that we can relegate our Longview Jerky T-shirts to the archives and replace them with the cheerful image of Clem T. Gofur.

All in all, it's good to see our dioramas again, although part of the point of adding this to our itinerary was so Richard could see what all the fuss was about and join in the hilarity—and he's not even here! We entertain ourselves for a good, long time in the van talking about donating a diorama to the Museum. Shakespeare seems the obvious choice. Gophers depicting a scene from Hamlet? Or MacBeth? Or perhaps something slightly more contemporary. A gopher diorama depicting the climactic scene from *Streetcar Named Desire*. Clem T. Gofur hanging drunkenly over a balcony bellowing "Stella"?

We decide this is definitely a project for our tenth anniversary tour.

And now to a sad but necessary interlude. Somehow these moments of tragic disillusionment always have to do with food, and memories of food, and our attempt to relive said memories. Sigh. Remember the Mennonite restaurant in Three Hills, Alberta? Remember the pie and pyrogies and roast turkey church-goers' lunch? In the scratch and sniff edition of this book, you too will be able to experience the rhapsody of eau de fresh-outa-the-oven. You too could cherish the memory . . .

We pull up in front of the Three Hills restaurant at about 4 PM. It's quiet. Too quiet. Not a half-ton in sight. We maintain our cheerful demeanor—all the more pie for us! Or, isn't that great we've missed that irritatingly busy farmers-in-town coffee hour? We pile out of the van and in through the front door of the restaurant. It's dark. But seconds later the proprietor scurries into the dining room from the kitchen area. He smiles, welcoming us as he flips on some lights, but he ain't no Mennonite baking queen. He looks like a cheerful and competent Chinese–Canadian restaurateur—is it too much to hope that he might be a pastry chef, too?

Bob is already muttering balefully. Tyler looks tearful. I ask, in a voice quavering with emotion, "Do you have pie?" Our host smiles, but of course. He ushers us to a table and disappears to make coffee. Should we stay? Shrugs all around as we pull out our chairs. We're a brave and plucky little crew. We peruse the menu in funereal silence. Bob slams his shut. "I suppose someone should risk it, but it sure as hell isn't going to be me."

"Says here there's coconut cream pie . . . ," I say tremulously. "Yeah, right. Made by that old ho Sara Lee," snaps Bob.

Our host returns with freshly made swill. We politely inquire about the pie, and several of us order a slice, hoping, praying . . . We hear the hum of the microwave in the background. Never a good sign. The pie arrives . . . we taste.

Human hands never mixed this filling or formed this pastry. This was made by some robot in a factory far, far away . . .

Stephen's cutlery clatters to the table. Patti pouts prettily as she pokes at her pie. Norma sniffles, dourly dabbing her pursed lips with a napkin. Brian sobs—operatically. Bob stomps out of the restaurant for a smoke. I soldier on, eating the slightly chemical-tasting foam topping my tart. Robert skates the pastry around his plate in an unconvincing display of appetite. Tyler excuses himself to go to the men's room and never comes back. (We'll find him later, wandering through a ditch picking wildflowers, humming a tuneless version of the "Torrington Gopher Call Song.")

Three Hills Lament
Who makes our dream pie?
Mennonites
Not slut Sara Lee

We pay up and politely thank our host. Pile into the van and drive south on Highway 21. Then pick up Highway 27 west and drive through grey, sullen landscapes toward the promise of happier culinary events.

The Porcine Papillion.

FIFTEEN

HAPPIER CULINARY EVENTS

The PaSu Farm is about forty-five minutes northwest of Calgary, reasonably close to the small town of Carstairs. The owners are a husband and wife team, Patrick and Sue de Rosemond, originally from South Africa, who came to Canada to escape the political situation in their homeland. Mrs. PaSu confides to us that while overall they've found Alberta to be hospitable, they were distressed after their arrival to have some folks compliment them on South Africa's apartheid policy as a great way of dealing with a "problem." She also says that her attempts to teach a yoga class in the area were met with suspicion in some quarters, as all that bending and stretching and breathing was considered by some to be the devil's work.

These interesting bits of social history are related in the PaSu Farm's gift shop, where Mrs. PaSu runs the store. (We were invited to come early for our dinner reservation in order to do a bit of SHOPPING. HA!) The primary focus of the gift shop is wool and sheepskin products, with some skincare products and African art thrown in for good measure. After a flurry of trying on sweaters and shawls my charge card and I escape mostly unscathed but every single one of the guys buys a heavy cotton shirt-coat in either gray or khaki green. They look cute as bugs wearing their purchases. Lined up in a row for a photo, they also look a bit like they could be Chairman Mao's garden crew.

After whetting our appetite with spending in the gift shop, we're ushered into the dining room for the main event. Our numbers are small, with only three tables settling in for tonight's feast. We're seated in front of enormous floor to ceiling windows that look out over the farm . . .

. . . revealing a scene of bucolic splendour. Gently rolling green hills. Neatly delineated fields. A few emus. Some cattle. And a number of cute fluffy little lambs. Frolicking, it has to be said. They have that charming, irresistible bounce in their step that all baby animals seem to have. Two of the little fellows play on a hillock right in front of our window. One scales the gentle slope; his friend joins him on the summit. They jostle for a few seconds and then tumble down the little hill. Lamb A seems to nuzzle Lamb B affectionately before they begin the whole game again, oblivious to their fate as our dinner. Only a dedicated and hard-hearted carnivore could contemplate this scene and think about racks of . . .

We sip our martinis and joke about picking our dinner out of the pasture, like choosing a lobster out of a tank in a seafood restaurant. This amuses us for a while until we're distracted by the first course: Terrine de Canard a la Orange with Port Wine jelly and Melba Toast. Yum.

> *Terrine de Canard*
> *Retail Splurge*
> *Will Visa Forgive*

(2005 and we still haven't figured out the damn haiku rules.)

The next time I look out the window all the lambs have mysteriously disappeared. Hmm . . .

> *Lamb bleats in sad grief*
> *No mint sauce*
> *His brother was racked*

Oh what a feast! The opening number is followed by "Maharaja Apple Soup," a creamy creation delicately flavoured with curry. Spinach Salad dressed with warm gorgonzola, raspberry and walnut Vinaigrette. Passion Fruit Sorbet. And—and—and—

While describing scenery in a pornographic vein feels somewhat stilted, food porn feels entirely natural and flows trippingly from the tongue. (I can still remember the taste of that soup!) I'm thinking that writing menus for restaurants—terrine de blah-blah, with a soupcon de blah-blah—might be almost as satisfying as foreplay. Speaking of which . . .

After all that delicious vamping, the main course arrives. Rack of Alberta Lamb. Veggies. Some sort of starch. A silence descends on the table.

> *Lambs frolic in fields*
> *Baa ram ewe*
> *We savour their racks*

We finish with Crème Caramel, Robert's favourite dessert. The menu for the evening is accompanied by a charming message from our hosts. Not an apologia, exactly. More like a manifesto. Including:

> *We have contemplated our situation in the food service industry and have decided that in essence we are definitely not offering a regular restaurant. Unlike City or Town restaurants we are not situated on a convenient corner waiting for someone to walk in the door and demand to be fed. Also, we do not suffer the vagrancies of a capricious dining clientele very well. Furthermore, we are not a standardized eatery.*

The Gals aren't sure what any of this means, especially "suffering vagrancies." The Gals don't really care—we've been fed and watered in fine style. The Chef emerges from the kitchen to visit with guests and accept kudos. I'd be delighted to fawn over him, only he has a huge, apricot-coloured parrot riding on his shoulder. I am really not a fan of birds. My stomach lurches as the smiling Chef makes his way toward our table. He sees the expression on my face and veers off.

I confide in the waitress that I'm a little queasy around birds. She rolls her eyes, says she doesn't particularly like the parrot either. (And he doesn't like her.) She reports that often when they have a full house, and are bringing out all the main courses on trolleys, the parrot flaps around the dining room trumpeting "baa-baa-baa" as he swoops over the lamb. Aaaaaakkkk!

With dinner and our gift shop purchases taken into account we reckon we've spent about a thousand dollars. A perfectly delightful evening, one of our best Saturday nights ever. Then to sleep and dreams of . . . bacon.

We have our best diner breakfast so far in the Didsbury Hotel in Didsbury, Alberta. Great coffee, cheesy omelettes, crispy toast—potato pancakes! Cheery, spectacular, mind-reading service. We charge out of the hotel extremely well-pleased and entirely oblivious to the drama about to unfold.

None of us have been watching the television for news or we'd probably know that the area we're headed for is in the throes of one of the worst floods of its history. (Environment Canada deems Alberta's June flooding as the top weather story of the year.) As we proceed north and west toward Sundre we see evidence everywhere that the rainfall has been too much for the Red Deer River. The water is lapping up over the edges of the James River Bridge. There's a trailer from a nearby (flooded) campground which is now floating down the river!

> *Raging water rises*
> *Trailers float*
> *Breakfast sure was good*

Also from the scrapbook:

Man's inhumanity to man never ceases to amaze me. As our fellow Albertans suffer the raging waters of the terrible floods of 2005 my fellow travel companions can only make insensitive remarks. What if they were searching Canadian Tire for a sump pump today? Sad, really. I wonder what's for lunch. I could have a nice clubhouse sandwich. Thank you.

There are actually several short essays along these lines (destruction everywhere and the Gals just eat) in the scrapbook. Oh well. Somehow we managed to overcome our guilt.

Just moments into Caroline we see signs for the Caroline and District Museum. The tiny building adjacent to a restored schoolhouse features artifacts from settler days. When we ask about the Kurt Browning museum reportedly housed at the town arena, our hosts, (Lil and Agnes? Beth and Betty?) hasten to inform us proudly that *they* have some Kurt Browning artifacts as well. Am I imagining things, or have we happened on a territorial dispute that hasn't been completely smoothed over?

There is the usual collection of clippings tracing Kurt's ascent to stardom. (An unfailingly classy guy and brilliant athlete, he deserves all the accolades he's received and more.) Turns out the good ladies of the Caroline Museum don't have any skates or medals or stretchy sequined pants, but they do have . . . Kurt's first suitcase. They proudly display this artifact, pointing out stickers on the battered, hard-sided case. We try to imagine Kurt's suitcase in faraway places, packed full of tighty-whities and big dreams.

From the scrapbook:

Best Historical Relic Seen on the Intolerance Tour: an oxen cart made by Pinky Pitts for Fred McNutt

We find the Caroline Arena, but sadly, the Browning museum ("Kurt's Korner") is closed. No photo ops, no T-shirts, no souvenir lycra-spandex jumpsuits.

> *Robert's Lament Haiku*
> *Kurt Browning's Corner*

Caroline
Skating Pants Denied

And now for the intolerance part of our tour. Word is, Terry Long owns a lumberyard in Caroline. We drive around in a somewhat desultory fashion, pretending to look for it. Really, we have absolutely nothing in mind here. We certainly have no interest in meeting this person, or anyone like him. I'm not sure what we'd do if we even found his lumberyard. Maybe we're curious about how the rest of the community views him, how someone who seems to us to be so outside the mainstream could be living some kind of regular life. Dunno—but the aimless and futile nature of this pilgrimage somehow amuses us.

Eventually we give up on this extremely modest travel objective. Maybe he lives here, maybe he doesn't. Maybe everyone shuns him at the diner and hardware store—maybe they think he's a great guy. We'll never know . . .

Now we make an unscheduled stop at the Dickson Dam. We join a crowd of gawkers at the top of the Dam to watch the roiling water pour over the huge concrete structure and flood the plains below. Unbelievable! It's a truly gobsmacked-by-nature moment. Horrific and riveting.

Wicked overflow
Dickson Dam
She's one mad mo-fo

Lunch at Spruce View. (According to the scrapbook, the scene of some imagined love triangle between Patti, the waitress and me. Possibly inspired by the fact that we initially misheard our waitress's claim to being a "thespian.") Then off to Eckville. This Intolerance Tour moment is much more inanely cheerful. We find Eckville High School and take endless photos of the group pointing at the sign. This is more our style, an entirely lame initiative pursued (and achieved). We're fascinated—and horrified—at the thought that those students from the eighties weren't necessarily fully deprogrammed after their time with Mr. Keegstra.

The scrapbook includes a list of interview questions to be posed to ex-students should we encounter them.

1. When I say six million, what do you automatically think of?
2. Could you possibly deny that there are eight people in this van?
3. How important was it to be popular at Eckville High School in 1982?

I neglect to mention to the Gals that I have a little tiny streak of this kind of thinking in my very own family. I remember very clearly my uncle Roy—may he rest in peace—pounding the table and saying this was all a "freedom of speech" issue. In his mind, Keegstra was some kind of hero. While I've never met anyone else who shared Keegstra's extreme views, I have met people who cautiously allowed that whatever else you might think of Keegstra (who owned a garage as well as teaching high school), he was a "damned hard worker." In this neck of the woods, that's right next to godliness.

The final stop on our tour is Sylvan Lake, Alberta. I have wonderful memories of coming here for the occasional booze-up whilst in high school. There was a historic, pre-war dance hall on the main drag. (Both my mother and Brian's went to "jitney dances" there during the war.) There was a French fries stand open right across the street from the beach, and exotic boys from the big old town of Red Deer, and drinking—and driving—and adolescent hormones and all that really great stuff.

Now Sylvan Lake is a rock'em-sock'em summer community, with all the lakeside properties bought up and developed by rich Calgarians. One of the few remnants remaining of a by-gone age is the famous Sylvan Lake Steam Baths. This is the planned climax of our 2005 Intolerance Tour. But it's just too hot and we're too tired. We drink beer at a sidewalk café. We eat some ice cream. We settle up and call it a weekend . . .

> Driving north as five
> And missing
> Our Calgary friends

Nature can be one mad mo-fo.

PHOTO: BOB ERKAMP

SIXTEEN

TRACING THE FUR TRADERS' ROUTE

This year marked a change of direction for the Gals. I mean, really—we blew our chance to celebrate Alberta's hundredth birthday. We could have been doing Centennial puppet shows out of the back of the van. We could have formed our own Centennial Marching Band! (I have always, always wanted to twirl a baton.) All over the province, people were taking a step back and saying wow . . . a hundred years, huh? Let's examine where we came from, where we're going as a province, as a people . . .

Meanwhile the Gals were careening down muddy back roads, dodging flood waters and looking for their next meal. Tsk, tsk—time to get serious.

When the notion was proposed that we could investigate and experience some of the early fur-trading history of the province, the Gals jumped at the chance. What I mean is, we soberly and earnestly considered the options, and carefully planned an educational tour through Alberta's past. Okay, that never happened. But I invite you to join with me in envisioning an alternate Buffalo Gals universe . . .

Friday night: The Buffalo Gals are all pretty darned excited about learning about the Fur Traders and their adventures. We begin our educational journey by gathering together in a seminar room at the University of Alberta for a lecture about fur trading economies. We're all amazed to discover what an impact the European demand for luxury fur items had on seventeenth century trading culture. We break for coffee and excitedly trace voyageur routes on a map mounted on the wall near the blackboard. Then back to the seminar on "tongue and groove" construction. Tyler makes an origami York boat for the instructor, to thank her for her inspiring presentation.

9:30 PM. Off to bed, we've got a big day tomorrow.

Saturday: After a simple breakfast of fruit and herbal tea, we hit the road and head north from Edmonton, all of us wearing our period costumes. We feel so authentic in our buckskin and bonnets, and attract quite a lot of attention when we stop at all the historical viewpoints along the side of the highway. Of course we read each write-up carefully, then hurry back to the van for discussion and questions. (Everyone's pretty eager to get to the hide-tanning workshop at the Lac La Biche Mission.) Finally Stephen absolutely insists on some journal time. We stop at a campsite and everyone slips away to a private spot while they record their impressions of the journey so far.

Private spot? Heeeeehhhheeeehhheee. Where's your private spot? Heeeeee . . .

Saturday, 10:30 AM. A reprimand is issued in order to keep this kind of puerile humour under wraps, but it meets with little success. It isn't long before the entire noble enterprise has deteriorated into fart jokes and drinking games.

Saturday, 1 PM. The van is returned to the rental agency and the Gals are sent home.

And I wake up. Thank heavens, it was all a dream . . .

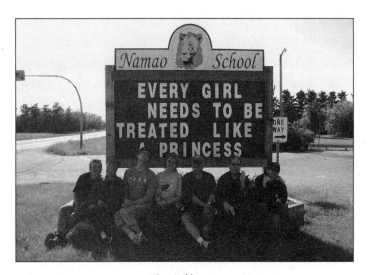

Irresistible . . .

PHOTO: PATTI PON

SEVENTEEN
PREPARING THE PELT

As per tradition, planning for this year's trip began in the van during June 2005. The dates were firmed up at the Buffalo Gals planning breakfast held during Blitz Weekend (the wrap-up of Alberta Theatre Projects' annual festival of new plays), also according to tradition. Musing about route and meal stops continues during the frenzy of planning emails in May. Unlike those early footloose and free-wheeling years, the Buffalo Gals weekend is now prescribed by a series of dearly-held, closely adhered-to rules of engagement.

1. We kinda like to come up with the theme for the following year's tour by the Sunday afternoon of the previous year.

2. Those of us who are able to come to Blitz Weekend—and it's always the same crew—like to have breakfast together on the Saturday morning, Day-timers and Blackberries in hand, to nail down a date.

3. Accommodations and tour highlights are discussed via email between March and June.

4. First night of the road trip we have a big dinner.

5. We spend as much money as possible.

6. We eat beef and bacon.

7. We document our impressions in the scrapbook. Most of the content is destined to be completely incomprehensible by the following year.

Simple, huh? It's a good working formula for serial road tripping. You *can* try this at home! (Again, I refer you to Appendix I.)

Since 2006 was definitely a year for a northern swing, tracing the fur traders' route seemed a perfect fit. It was a classic Buffalo Gals theme: just enough reality to provide a context for our riffing and razzing and the loose organization of an itinerary, and yet lots of potential for events and places to be um, er, underwhelming.

Perhaps we're at a point in our history when it doesn't much matter where we go or what we do. We need to be on the move and we need to eat. Nothing else seems to matter. That said, we always put on a great show of actually planning a trip.

DATE: May 6, 2006

FROM: Me

Hey cowpies and girls! A few items of interest . . .

Athabasca was the "gateway to the great north country" from 1880 to 1914. The road from Edmonton to Athabasca was called the Athabasca Landing Trail! Fur traders used to stock up at the Perryvale General Store or stop and skin a raccoon at Colinton. Both on our route.

In Lac La Biche there's the Lac La Biche Mission and they do role-playing and such. Sounds like just the thing for a bunch of show folks. There's also something called the Kak Ki Yaw Cultural Camp where you can learn to portage or something. (I'll leave you to do some googling on the latter two attractions.)

LUX—pish-posh steak house for Friday night? Or are we off beef this year? HAHAHA

PS: Ben says their neighbour at the cabin is a TRAPPER! Think of the seminar we could have.

How many days till the trip, Patti??

DATE: May 8, 2006
FROM: Norma
TO: Gals

So where do we get our Metis belt things so we have something to hold our firearms and such! And can we wear fur hats? And what did the fur traders wear? Can we get a York boat, launch it onto the North Saskatchewan then paddle to Athabasca? I'm sure there is one lying around Fort Edmonton. I know there were ones used during the filming of that famous movie made in Alberta "Marie Ann"—the story of the grandmother of Louis Riel. (The first white woman to arrive in the west at Fort Edmonton.) She was the beginning of the end for the fur trade because it meant that once the families arrived, all the guys would have to give up their Indian "wives" and start to settle down, thus leading to the establishment of towns in Alberta. Anyway the story goes something like that. More later.

DATE: May 12
FROM: Brian
TO: Gals

Hey, wasn't there some talk of dressing up Patti like Pocahontas?

ON 5/12/06 Patti wrote:
Yeah, right buddy—whatever makes the road trip feel more authentic to the rest of you freaks.

DATE: Friday, May 26, 2006
FROM: Me
TO: Gals
SUBJECT: Eight Sleeps to Pelt
Okay I've already decided that Norma should be our historical anima-teur so that's settled. But there's many other questions . . .

    1. When does Stephen and Tyler's flight get in? (I think everyone should feel free to guess but only two pelters know the answer.)

    2. Are you Calgary folks okay to bunk with us on Friday night? We have a double futon, Brian has room for Patti (she'll curl up under Brian's pillow) and another two folks on his futon. Richard has room for one.

3. There's a deluxo steak house here we're keen to try. (They hang their beef.) Or we can eat in the Selkirk Hotel at Fort Edmonton. Will check out the latter as the thematic resonance appeals. And Norma will assign costume pieces. I will certainly wear a bonnet which also acts as a backsplash for steak juices.

4. As far as I know we're still on for Laurie and Ben's cabin. Will confirm today and find out what the bedding situation is. Oh Lord, we don't really want to be putting sleeping bags in our little van do we???!!

5. Itinerary. I'm not sure we really have one but there are a couple of routes we can take and there's a hot tub at the end of the day so nothing else matters. Oh yeah—add TOWEL and TRUNKS to your list.

What else? Oh—I just realized we can leave town by means of Fort Road and thus go by "Bob's Sausage House." Best jerky anywhere.

SMOOCHES—LOOKING FORWARD TO YOUR FEEDBACK!

On 5/26/06 Brian wrote:
Bob's SAUSAGE house? I can already imagine Tyler's haiku!

DATE: May 26, 2006
FROM: Stephen
SUBJECT: Hanging their Beef?!
So the answer to every question this year could be "Bob's Sausage" as opposed to "James Keegstra." Norma are we bringing our own fur-trading outfits or do you have a source? Will you be wearing that smart High River hat again with the Minnie Pearl price tag?

Can't wait to see the PELT T-shirts. I am, however, bringing the entire Buffalo Gals Collection.

XXXXXXXXX Vancouver Boys

FROM: Bob
TO: Gals
What happened to staying at the Fort Edmonton thing? I was pumped! And we're pretty excited about Patti's guest appearance as Pocahontas, too.

Yes, please—bedding at the cabin. We don't have sleeping bags and have no intention of ever buying them.

You will note that no one except Norma gives a big flying frigging crap about any of the historical stuff.

This year, for the very first time, the Gals had custom-designed T-shirts—hurray. Our dear Richard took on this duty and supplied us with a truly striking article of clothing. A basic black T-shirt with pillowy orange text proclaiming the name of our tour: PELT!

PELT!
Feel the magic . . . be the experience . . .
Tour 2006
. . . 10 people . . . 4 wheels . . . one chance to change the world!!!
Calgary Edmonton Ponoka Leduc Lacombe Perryvale Athabasca
Colinton Lac La Biche Kak ki Yaw Beaver Lake Bruderheim
Calgary Edmonton Ponoka Leduc Lacombe Perryvale Athabasca
Colinton Lac La Biche Kak ki Yaw Beaver Lake Bruderheim
Calgary Edmonton Ponoka Leduc Lacombe Perryvale Athabasca
You Pelt 'er You Brought 'er Colinton Lac La Biche Kak ki Yaw
Beaver Lake Bruderheim Calgary Edmonton Ponoka Leduc
Lacombe Perryvale Athabasca Colinton Lac La Biche Kak ki
Yaw Beaver Lake Bruderheim

—T-shirt inscription

We are absolutely totally beyond tickled pink to be wearing our specially designed team uniforms. We have many happy hours in the van coming up with different meanings for the acronym PELT. To be honest, this might not have occurred to us except that everywhere we go, people ask us what PELT stands for.

Punish Elephants Leaving Turds!
Peace Everywhere Let's Talk
People Eating Leftover Turkey

The other element that enriches our experience this year is that some wise soul figures out the scansion of haiku and brings this valuable information to the attention of the group. This new and vital intelligence triggers an outpouring of poetic expression in the scrapbook.

> *Pickled pelt is gross*
> *But wait jerked beef has merit*
> *Oh contradiction*
> *We even explore some different poetic forms*
> *On a trip to the north of the land*
> *We all gathered in one merry band*
> *Tho we had much to drink*
> *No one threw up in the sink*
> *And by morning we were all feeling grand.*
> *As we traveled past field after field*
> *Our thoughts and our drama were revealed*
> *We wrote through our tears*
> *And exposed all our fears*
> *That the Haiku were always properly metered*
> *For her photos before her we bow*
> *She's a true Buffalo Girlie and how!*
> *So one must use the correct forma*
> *When retrieving our Norma*
> *Get back in the Goddamn Van—NOW!*
> *Her pelt spotted with jerky and wurst*
> *One might think our poor Conni'd been cursed*
> *But each sight gives her pleasure*
> *To inordinate measure*
> *So from now on, we'll just pet her first.*

Okay, "poetic expression" might be pushing it. In fact, good taste prevents me from relating most of the content of this year's scrapbook. Honestly, the quality of the reportage has declined in recent years, but this year we tumble down to a new low. The content is mostly rude limericks, unrepeatable (or simply inexplicable) haiku and some wrappers from some of our van treats. Still, once in a while the Gals rise to the occasion.

> *History prevails*
> *Beaver, coon and mighty moose*
> *Pelt! Feel the magic*

So as they say, let the magic begin . . .

Pelts!

PHOTO: PATTI PON

EIGHTEEN
PELTI

PRESENT:
Everyone
ABSENT:
Not a soul

Friday, June 2

The Gals one and all—TEN of us, our biggest tour ever, ever—gather at our house for margueritas. These Friday night cocktail hours are important, as people need to work out the kinks before they can properly enjoy the weekend. That mostly consists of mushy greetings, drinks, and catch-up on work and family. All this has to be cleared off the agenda before we get down to business.

We pack up the van and make the long journey to the first stop on the road trip: Fort Edmonton Park.

Fort Edmonton, nestled on the south bank of the North Saskatchewan River, is a "living history park" featuring the restored

1846 Hudson Bay Company Fort, 1885 Street, 1905 Street, and 1920 Street. It's big—one hundred and fifty-eight acres—and staffed by scores of interpreters in historical costumes who help you play make-believe as you wander through the park. You can ride around the premises in various old-tyme conveyances: steam engine train, antique vehicles, horse-drawn carts. You can watch the settlers and townsfolk go about their business baking bread or fixing harness. You can even play 1920s-style miniature golf!

The Hotel Selkirk was an important part of civilized life in Edmonton at the turn of the last century. The clientele of the Hotel were strictly A-list—doesn't that sound like the Gals?—and the Hotel's Mahogany Room contained Canada's longest bar. (Oh, that's sooooo Albertan.) The Hotel burned down in 1962, but this beautiful replica looks authentic as all get-out.

We're slated for a three-course dinner in Johnson's Café, followed by a cozy sleep in the rooms upstairs. Hurray! The meal is lovely, though I'm happy that the only other party in the dining room is a largish group wrapping up a conference. (I try to imagine a couple having a romantic dinner anywhere close to our big, loud table of insanely excited and enthusiastic diners wearing matching T-shirts with puffy orange writing, and I shudder.) We hoot and holler, yell things down the length of the table, and convince one of the staff to lend us her white, starched hat so we can each wear it for a commemorative photo. *She* looks like a beautiful servant on the Titanic; *we* look like deranged Amish settlers.

Happily our neighbours in the dining room make at least as much noise as us. Things even get friendly between our tables later in the evening, especially when one of their lot asks what the acronym "Pelt" stands for. Stephen makes up something on the spot (Something vaguely credible-sounding to do with "learning" . . . ?) And now we're off and running, playing with our acronym. Did I ever say we weren't easily entertained?

We mow our way through all the courses and finally, when it's exceedingly clear that the only thing between the staff and their well-earned rest is our presence, we go outside for a stroll. It's a beautiful summer night. Them that smokes light 'em up, and we wander up and down 1885 and 1905 streets. It's a bit like walking through a ghost town, or like having a theme park all to yourself, after hours.

We have breakfast at the Hotel—part of the great package deal we've scored that includes last night's dinner and the room—and decide we'll delay our departure from Edmonton in order to spend a couple of hours puddling around the park. We nearly lose Norma five or ten times as she's seriously interested in all the history here. ("Norma—no—get out of the York boat—it's a three-hour tour!") There is a ride on the trolley, and on a horse-drawn wagon, and finally on the steam engine train. We see a couple of students we recognize from the BFA Acting program at the University of Alberta, dressed up in period costumes. What a lovely, gentle summer gig . . .

There's talk of getting some proper coffee as no one feels like they got properly stoked up in the dining room this morning. I open my big mouth and say that the best cup of coffee in Edmonton can be had at a little Italian joint in the university area. So off we go—it takes us several minutes to park the big, unwieldy van in this very busy area of town, another half an hour to get ten people sorted out with their lattes and cappuccinos and americanos and such.

Just as we're finally leaving Brian runs into a student from an opera training program currently in session a couple blocks away at the university. Brian's one of the instructors in the program; in fact he's meant to be teaching this kid a class right now. (He rearranged the schedule so he could be on the road trip instead.) Hilariously, he has to explain to this guy why it's early afternoon of the second day and we still haven't left town . . .

Now, the final and most burningly important stop before we bust loose from city limits: Bob's Sausage House. This is like a mini Roots tour for Robert. (He grew up in this end of the city.) Bob's Sausage House was the butcher of choice for his parents, and years later Robert discovered Bob's beef jerky.

The tiny, one-storey stucco building with an unassuming sign sits on Fort Road, a major thoroughfare in Edmonton that lends access to some hideous industrial real estate and notorious drinking holes (like the Transit Hotel). No one at Bob's Sausage House has gone out of the way to pretty up the inside of the premises either. You got yer one big glass case, full of raw meat. An old yellowed chart on the wall, showing different cuts of beef. And the place hasn't been painted in many a long year. As we enter, a well-heeled customer is at the counter asking about some special sausage. Bob (the butcher) is sold out; Butcher Bob's not all that reassuring about when the next batch will be ready. The customer leaves, obviously disappointed.

A small drama: it had never occurred to us that we wouldn't be able to get the jerky. We inquire, breath bated. Yippee—they've got it—we clean them out of their supply. The clerk stuffs big brown paper bags with large slabs of jerky. (No one's gone out of the way to pretty up the packaging here, either.) We spend a surprising amount of money on this snack item (about seventy dollars?) but it's worth it—the jerky is really, really good. I don't know how they make jerky—I don't wanna know—but it seems like it would be a pretty terrific thing to carry in your knapsack if you were about to snowshoe through the forest. Or go on a long hunting trip. Or walk for miles to get to the Fort to sell your furs. High, quality, delicious protein. So yeah, like, we're buying the jerky because it's thematically on point. Yeah, that's it. Not because it's another way of consuming BEEF.

Phew! We're finally out of town. We drive for about an hour and a half, stroll around Legal, an extremely charming little town with French-Canadian flourishes here and there, and some delightful public art. (Murals, giant folk art sculpture.) We buy pop and chips at the grocery store on Main Street and get ready to vamoose. But this time it seems we've finally done it—we've lost Norma. We confer, who saw her last? We check out several businesses. We drive up and down Main Street in the van, slowly, and with faces pressed to windows. Finally we spot her, wandering dreamily down a side street, camera in hand . . .

Okay, so far nothing on the trip has been lame, right? Everything has been perfectly lovely, just as we might have dreamed and even better. But now . . .

Somewhere in my admittedly half-arsed research, I was sure I read that Perryvale was one of the stops on the fur traders' Athabasca Landing Trail. And that there was a charming old-tyme General Store to mark the spot. With handmade crafts. The Gals, ever alert to the possibility of a retail opportunity, are keen to take the side trip off Highway 2 North.

It's quite a little adventure getting there. And when we arrive . . . "there" is nowhere, really. Perryvale consists of a store, basically, with hardly any stock. The "handmade crafts" consist of one crocheted toilet paper cover. One of the Gals (me?) buys a can of pop thinking this might entitle us to use the bathroom. Sure—we're welcome to use the outhouse across the street.

There's unrest out by the van: Bob is muttering darkly as he puffs malevolently on his third or fourth smoke of this pit stop. Brian looks downcast. Tyler wanders off and moos mournfully at a skinny cow grazing listlessly in a nearby pasture. Norma sits in the back of the van reading—there's absolutely nothing here that tickles her photographic imagination. Only glass-half-full Stephen has maintained an upbeat demeanor. The last one in the store, he tells the owner about our pilgrimage/road trip and she sends out a handful of souvenir pens for the group. This cheers us up. A little.

Some Edmonton friends who have a cabin on Lawrence Lake (about an hour north of here), have agreed to let us stay there for the night. We decide we better find the place while it's still light, i.e., before we go into Athabasca for dinner. After a bit of the inevitable back and forthing over the same stretch of the highway, looking for the landmarks referred to in the directions, we find the cabin. It's actually more of a compound, with a couple of different buildings and a little shed called Butch's Hideaway. Utterly charming and with a great view of the lake. There's a fireplace and a hot tub and great paperback novels strewn around. I think we're all tempted to run away from our lives and just stay here forever. But we must forage for food.

Athabasca seems to have several eating establishments that would do the trick. We opt for the classic small-town steak and pizza establishment. This place has a distinctly Italian flavour, so most of us just go with that. Spaghetti and meatballs. Spaghetti and steak. Only Richard has an extremely unhappy event in connection with food. I know that sounds precious ("Sir Pilkington really did prefer the ostrich.") but no kidding, this was bad. The "dressing" on his Caesar salad was a huge dollop of barbecue sauce. And that was only the beginning of Richard's bad luck on this trip . . .

It's a pleasantly low-key evening. A few of us walk up to the Burger Bar for soft ice cream, then stroll along the waterfront before returning to the cabin. Several of us enjoy the hot tub; it's only lukewarm but has a lovely view of the lake at the bottom of the cabin's front yard. Kevin builds (and tends) a cozy fire. Brian pops popcorn. The badinage is lazy and mild-mannered.

I just want to say, for the record, that I have absolutely no idea how Robert and I ended up on a comfy bed in the main cabin right beside the only flush toilet on the premises. No idea. None. I feel especially bad after hearing about my friends crashing through the underbrush in the middle of the night to use the outdoor biffy. I'm truly heart-broken that Richard found a dead mouse in his bed. Really, though, I don't know how me being uncomfortable would help Richard deal with bad salad, the dead rodent, or the moth floating in his Sunday morning tea.

> *A darkened cabin*
> *Pull the sheets over my head*
> *Powdered mice between my toes*

We have morning coffee sitting on the patio looking out at the lake, then we clean the cabin. And let me tell ya, we clean hard, as all of us are sorta frightened of one of the co-owners of the cabin, a brilliant and somewhat ferocious Liberal MLA.

Breakfast—and man we are hungry enough to tear the head off a collie—at the Green Spot Restaurant in Athabasca. ("Mom, Mom, I had a great time at the G Spot!") We're so completely out of our minds when the food finally arrives that the whole table bursts into spontaneous applause. But soon we're full of coffee and toast and bacon, and eager to experience all the magnificent historical experiences lined up for the day. We charge off to the Lac La Biche Mission for a great big dose of Alberta history.

The Lac La Biche Mission (Notre Dame des Victoires) was officially established in 1853 as a supply depot, and became one of the first Albertan sites for exchanges between the Native, Metis, Francophone, and Anglophone populations. The Oblate Missionaries, the Grey Nuns, and the Daughters of Jesus built schools, grew all their own food, and educated the Metis and Native children in the area. Or, according to the website, they "built this mission to be the root of colonization through their devotion in education, healthcare and commitment toward the population of Northern Alberta and Western Canada."

The website also promises guided tours and period role-playing!

We're actually quite excited by the time we get to the Mission. (Especially Norma.) We enter the main building, giggling and shoving each other like a bunch of kids on a high school field trip. The young man who greets us isn't as excited to see us as we are to see him. We tell him we're here for some period role-playing and a guided tour. Okay, maybe just a tour. And even though we have our wallets out, ready to pay, and we are the only living beings on site other than him and his colleague, he tells us he won't be doing a tour for another hour. The end.

Some mother's son badly needs a course in dealing with the public, and in Tourism 101, and basic common sense. It doesn't take much to make us happy. (As you've seen over and over again.) We've come quite a long way to see this place, but we must have interrupted a game of computer solitaire or something because buddy what's-his-name is definitely not interested in showing us around.

We kind of kick our tires for a little while after this disappointment. Richard and Tyler jump the fence and wander all around the Mission without the benefit of a tour. Bob and Robert stand by the van and smoke. Patti and Brian go exploring across the road and discover an old graveyard. (Is there anything sadder than a run-down graveyard?)

I join them there and we discover the grave of two children, with the name Catherine Parr Trail etched on the stone. Could it be the same Catherine Parr Trail, sister of Susanna Moodie, who wrote about her experiences as a pioneer? Surely not. Turns out the little ones were Catherine Parr Trail's grandchildren. (Her son worked in the fur trade here for a time.)

It takes us a very long while to round up the troupe at this venue, but finally we have our full complement, even Norma, and are ready to proceed into Lac La Biche, where more disappointment awaits.

Before the whining resumes, however, let me say what a spectacularly beautiful townsite this is. Starting with the name: Lac La Biche. Lovely, huh? Lac La Biche is one of the oldest communities in the province. The explorer David Thompson arrived here at 1 PM on October 4, 1798. As was his custom, the first thing he wrote in his journal was, "Thank God." The next comment in his journal might well have been "darned pretty."

As is *our* custom, we have a pretty loose agenda now that we're here, although we do have a couple of hot tips from a Red Deer College acting student who grew up here. "George" says we should head for "sweet beach" once we get to town. Email communication (and typos) being what they are, we're not entirely sure whether or not the beach is "Sweet Beach" (named after Bert and Ethel Sweet), or "Sweeeeet, man," George being twenty years old and all. We head for the sandy border along Lake Lac La Biche and it is lovely indeed. It's not quite hot enough to strip down and sunbathe, but we sit for a while and stare out at the water.

It's always interesting to note the group dynamics during these interludes when there's nothing particular on the agenda except a leg-stretch or a wander around the premises.

We've actually just had one of these at the Mission, where the Gals sort of buggered off in various directions, with no clear idea of when we'd report back to the van. Richard and Tyler tend to be the wander-off-and-smell-the-roses types. ("Oh look—a stick. Oh look, there's a doggy on the beach.") Bob, by contrast, gets bored very quickly if there's no structured activity planned. He'll make a perfunctory tour of the site in question (Yup, that's a beach), then light up a smoke. Maybe even have a second smoke leaning against the back door of the van. Eventually he'll just get back in the vehicle. As in "Get the hell back here and let's get on with the program."

Norma . . . well we know what Norma's doing, don't we? Patti and Kevin almost always seem to have reading material with them, so if the current situation is under-stimulating they can easily entertain themselves. Robert might have a smoke then stare off into space. Brian has a bit more trouble chilling out. (After all these years I still can't get him to take off his watch whilst on holiday.)

And me, well I suppose my role is to worry about group dynamics. Is everyone okay? Bob is looking crabby. I think he wants to move on. Stephen's gone, so is Brian. Oh, turns out they climbed the hill up from the beach and discovered the Lac La Biche Cultural Centre. Patti and Norma are walking down the beach—wait, I wanna come too! But Richard and Tyler are giggling about something—maybe they're having more fun. Where's Robert—is he having fun? He's smoking and sitting on a picnic table. He'd better not throw that cigarette butt on the lawn, that would drive me crazy. Everyone looks restless—oh no, actually the boys are still playing on the beach. What should we do next? This is our best road trip ever. Our worst road trip ever. Oh no, it's going to rain. I have to pee. I might be hungry. Is anyone else hungry?

Sigh. I can't help it—it's just the way I am. Am I painfully sensitive to social nuance? Or just a monkey brain extraordinaire. Mother hen on meth.

Eventually the balance tips and everyone starts to gather together again. Since we're still sort of trying to pursue this increasingly raggedy-ass agenda of fur-trading history and all, we decide to take a peek in the Lac La Biche Cultural Centre. Besides, there's bound to be bathrooms there.

It's quite a lovely building, with a few interesting artifacts from settlers and explorers and such. But by far the most interesting item is a six-inch solid silver ball made entirely of cigarette papers. Apparently it took local non-smoker Doreen Hunka over seven years to construct it. Wow . . . you have to wonder. Oh wait, there's a pretty young woman behind the counter. Perhaps she'll know more about this. I smile at said young woman and ask her if she knows why Doreen Hunka made the silver ball. (Surely there's a story behind this.) Young woman looks sort of irritated at the interruption. Answers, in her best Valley girl contemptuous lilt, "I have noooo idea." And goes back to her book.

Wow. Little missy went to the same how-to-deal-with-the public seminar that Lac La Biche Mission Man attended. I'm not sure but I think this is where we officially throw in the towel on our agenda to explore Alberta's settler past. (And anti-smoking activism?) Oh, except for the group photos we take around the lovely statue of David Thompson, set on a high point overlooking beautiful Lac La Biche.

It's almost time to turn the van around and point it in the direction of Edmonton. But there's one last thing on the agenda, inspired by our friend George. I hesitate to describe this incident, as it's certainly one of our dunderhead moments. But hey, I've committed to sort of telling the truth here, and you'll just have to trust me that we're normally really, really smart until we get in that van. So. George says there's a really great strawberry farm just outside of town. George says we absolutely have to go. We're pretty sure it's too early for strawberries, but maybe they grow them in a hothouse or something.

We drive out to Shady Lane Berry Farm, craving some success with at least one of our ventures today. (So far, breakfast is the only thing we've pulled off.) Stephen and I volunteer to get out of the van and make an enquiry. A beautiful young woman comes to the door, listens to our question, politely informs us that it's just a little early for strawberries. Subtext: "Let me guess, you idiots are city folks." Stephen and I mumble our thanks and scuttle back to the van.

PELT, Buffalo Gals VIII, does end on a high note, however. We have the settling supper at one of the best burger joints in Edmonton (The Garage), and decide for the first time that we should give everyone official responsibilities.

Me: President!

Robert: Transportation and IT

Patti: Diversity
Stephen: Treasurer and Archives
Tyler: Youth Coordinator and Pelt Wrangling (?)
Kevin: Catering and Choreography
Bob: Member Services
Richard: Image and Branding
Brian: Media
Norma: Security

All positions were decided by acclamation. The scrapbook wraps up with a list of recommendations for the following year.

> Suggestions for Next Year Tour #9 (composed by Tyler)
> Circulate the name of Conni's hairdresser
> Offer advance seat selection in the van
> Purchase and install GPS chip for Norma

Sunset at Lawrence Lake.
PHOTO: PATTI PON

NINETEEN
WHITHER GOEST GALS?

It's never a good sign when we don't have our theme for the following year's tour chosen, titled, and thoroughly chewed over by late Sunday of the previous year. We actually spent more time on Tour Number Eight riffing about our tenth anniversary than we did planning Tour Number Nine.

Norma has more than once made a pitch for us to go to Peace River Country. Many of us are keen but the conversation always stalls with someone among our number saying, "Well, of course we'd have to fly to Grande Prairie first." Brian has often expressed a desire to go to Fort McMurray, oil sands country. But we're generally agreed that while McMurray might be very interesting, there's not a whole hell of a lot to see on the route there and back. Tricky to have a road trip when there's no points of interest along the way.

There's also talk of heading to the mountains for a weekend. This makes me nervous. What's the theme? "We Be Big Fat Wilderness Trampling Tourists Too?" I'm worried that there's absolutely no cheese content in a trip like this, that it'll just be a couple of expensive dinners in the insanely—and heartbreakingly—busy town of Banff. Big whoop.

For a while we even have a theme but no itinerary. It came about one early winter evening in Edmonton. After a delightful and somewhat boozy dinner party a few of us were having a little rant about the state of arts funding in the province. Probably because, once again, the Alberta Foundation for the Arts had been stiffed in the latest budget. This in a province that had just posted a multi-billion dollar surplus. This in a province that subsidizes many other industries, especially the oil business, to the tune of millions of dollars. The politicians often polish their stump with speeches about jobs for "average Albertans" or "ordinary Albertans" (whom Premier Ralph Klein is fond of referring to as "Martha and Henry"). Let's get that heavy oil processing plant up and running, dammit, cause that's a boon to ordinary Albertans. But somehow people who work in cultural industries aren't considered "average Albertans"—maybe we're not even real. Or human.

Actually we're more like . . . court jesters. So removed from the needs and desires and dreams of regular folks that maybe they assume we'll just keep doing that crazy thing we do (act, write, sing) even if we're starving to death.

Out of this familiar and embittered rant that winter evening came the idea that no matter what, artists always have to "bark for treats." At the time that also seemed like a fun thing to put on a T-shirt. "Bark for Treats—Tour 2007." We weren't just exactly sure where that would take us. We weren't sure where to go, period. Surely, just for the sake of symmetry and all, we could squeeze out a couple more trips and make it to number ten. Or maybe we've exhausted ourselves, and our road trip concept—and the concept of living here in Alberta.

What ARE we doing here, anyway?

There are family issues to be sure. Robert, Brian, Richard, and I all have aging parents living nearby. In terms of career, there are very good arguments for living in Vancouver or Toronto. But I'm surprised at how much more important the considerations of climate and geography have become over the years.

It has occurred to me that I may never live anywhere else. (Unless you count retirement; I hope I'll someday have a little place in warmer climes.) I don't know how the other Gals feel about this. Brian will always wander, I imagine, but many of the other Gals are here for life as well. And I suspect Stephen and Tyler could be lured back. So what is it about our love–hate relationship with our chosen home? Maybe we love the contradictions:

We dream big, but we protect ourselves with healthy skepticism. We're independent spirits, but we have an unparalleled sense of community. Even as we're famous for going our own way, we're also nationally known for our volunteer spirit, joining together in great numbers to organize Olympic events, arts festivals, and emergency relief efforts.

Tension between these elements creates a kind of energy, I guess. A sort of enlivening hostility? Maybe that's a good thing. After all, everyone knows that drama requires conflict . . .

But this ain't drama; this is real life. I think we've established that we *embrace* the contradictions inherent in the Alberta experience. But the conflict? Maybe not so much. I am not the natural enemy of the farmer out by Wainwright just because I'm an artist. (We both take risks; we both toil on in the face of mysterious and temperamental market forces.) And we have seen over and over again on our trips that we are connected to our fellow Albertans in all the most essential ways: through landscape, family, and funny bones. There's no question that some of the Gals function outside the mainstream, and that we would certainly be out of our element chewing the fat with Farmer Jones at the local auction mart. But surely there's room for all of us— since everywhere you look there's space.

We didn't always have to bark for treats—the arts flourished under the Peter Lougheed Conservatives in the seventies and eighties. Then something shifted. Actually, I've heard more than one person speculate that the shift from Camelot to Calvary dates back to an event at Red Deer College in the early nineties, just before Ralph Klein's tenure began.

Three Deads in a Baggie, one of Canada's best-loved comedy troupes, was performing at a theatre conference in Red Deer. The

Trolls, renowned for their bawdy humour and hilarious improvisational outbursts, had been explicitly warned to keep their presentation clean, as Doug Main, minister of culture and multiculturism, and a prominent social conservative, would be in attendance with his wife. Apparently the Trolls didn't take too kindly to the suggestion about the content of their material. (What do you expect? Talk about inviting the anarchists to a picnic.) Apparently one of the troupe members punctuated one of the sketches with some full frontal nudity. And it's been all downhill ever since.

Maybe the Trolls did step over the line (oh how I wish I'd been there to see it) but you'd think they—we—could be forgiven the occasional indiscretion. After all, Albertans seemed to forgive Ralph Klein in December 2001, after he made a drunken, late-night visit to an Edmonton homeless shelter (the Herb Jamieson Centre), shouted and swore at some bewildered men to "get a job!" then threw some change on the floor as a final insult before leaving. In many areas of the world, this would signal the end of a public career. But somehow Ralph was able to spin this into a bonding moment with Martha and Henry. Aaak! This time I shout it to the heavens—why do we live here?

Well—if not here, where then? It seems every region of the country has its own breed of wonky politics. BC is beautiful, but its government is about as hospitable to artists as it is to homeless people. Manitoba seems to do things right, but it has the biggest mosquitoes in the world. The only province in the country that seems to truly celebrate its culture is Quebec, but I'm probably too unashamedly (mawkishly?) Canadian to live with the tension of the separatist agenda.

Maybe the real question is: does going on the road trip year after year make us feel better or worse about our lives here? I'm going to go out on a limb and say the road trip is a restorative tonic. Sort of the dead opposite of an artist's retreat, with all its exhausting, loud-mouthed hilarity and yet, I find it endlessly inspiring. During the time we've been going on these trips, I've written more about Alberta than I have in the rest of my career put together. So is the road trip experience fundamental to who we are as artists? Oh hell—who knows, really? All I can say is, the minute we leave the city and the view opens up on either side of the highway, something lifts inside of me.

By the time we meet for our traditional planning breakfast in March there's mass confusion about our road trip destination(s) and our theme.

Scene: A Calgary Diner

(Conni, Stephen, Patti, Bob, Kevin and Richard sit at a table together picking through the remains of their breakfast. Norma, who has just finished doing a PowerPoint presentation, distributes handouts.)

Norma: I urge you . . . I beseech you to seriously consider "Peace River Country—A Little Bit of Heaven in 2007." And thus I conclude my presentation. Thank you.

(Norma takes her seat, there's a smattering of applause.)

Conni: *(puzzling over the handout)* What is this anyway?

Norma: That's a biography of twelve-foot Davis. As well I've included some statistical information about the topography of the region. And a chart depicting average temperature and rainfall in the summer months.

Richard: *(raises his hand)*

Norma: Yes, Richard.

Richard: There's a hair in my hash browns.

Patti: You're a whiny one, ain't ya?

Richard: Well what does that look like to you?

Patti: It's not too late to replace you on the tour, bud.

(Richard sulks.)

Bob: So we fly to Grande Prairie . . .

Norma: Yes!

Stephen: But I thought we were going to Rosebud dinner theatre. Which would actually take us right past the PaSu sheep farm!

(GROANS all around.)

Kevin: I thought we were going to Banff.

(BEWILDERED MURMURING.)

Richard: Well I've never been to Lake Louise—or the Columbia Icefields—

Conni: The Icefields! That's it! It's time we dealt with the most serious concern currently facing the human race. It's time the Buffalo Gals confronted the Herculean conflict between man and nature; it's time we stepped up! Don't you think?

(The GALS are awed by my rhetoric. Except for Patti.)

Patti: (*looking at a brochure*) Or we could go to Reptile World in Drumheller.

Conni: Patti!

Well it was something like that, anyway. Once we happened upon the idea of visiting the Columbia Icefields and having a first-hand look at our disappearing glaciers, we were off to the races. The 2007 trip soon coalesced around a concept—environmentalism—and a title: AN INCONVENIENT TOUR.

We talked a great deal about visiting the ancestral home of Darrin Hagen in Rocky Mountain House since we'd be driving right by there. Darrin is an Edmonton treasure: drag queen, author, playwright, actor, and television host. He grew up in a trailer park in Rocky Mountain House (the inspiration for his very funny play

Tornado Magnet), and we thought maybe we could get Darrin to show us around the old hometown. Although, heaven knows, as we started to imagine what it must have been like growing up gay in Rocky Mountain House, we realized this event might have been more properly included on the "Intolerance Tour." Anyway, this item sort of fell off the agenda. Maybe eventually we'll have to do a "rebels and revolutionaries" road trip that would include the birthplaces of KD Lang and Darrin Hagen and Marshall McLuhan.

For now, though, we're sticking to our green tour objective. (Richard already has lots of ideas about the T-shirt design.) Seeing the Columbia Icefields at some point on the weekend will pretty much justify our existence. Everything else is gravy. Then it happens: an event so perfectly designed for Buffalo Gals consumption we can hardly believe our good fortune.

The Big Valley Creation Science Museum is set to open THREE DAYS before our road trip!! Yes oh yes—a "creationist" museum! What fun.

In recent years we have often been thwarted in our attempt to enjoy the traditional religious/sacrilegious component of our trip. (That's probably the real reason we were turned away from the Lac La Biche Mission last year.) This fascinating side trip to Big Valley (the roast beef dinner train trip destination from Tour 2002) may fit the bill.

There's no possible way the Creation Museum could be considered consistent with our environmental "Gals gone green" agenda. (Although maybe the fundamentalists consider creationism to be a very convenient truth indeed.) I have to say I argued for the Museum being included in some later edition of our tours. But certain Gals made a compelling argument that a) Big Valley, site of the museum, really wasn't that much out of our way; and b) who knows if the place would actually survive the winter? The decision made, we could then enjoy endless badinage in anticipation of the experience, most of it pretty brilliantly insightful and mind-bendingly thoughtful. (Except for Patti, who only wanted to know if there'd be T-shirts to buy.)

Other than that, most of the email preamble was about where we would eat and drink on Friday in Red Deer, our planned rendezvous point, and about T-shirt design.

Not everyone's excited about the proposed colour, an eye-popping neon green, but we all approve of the logo and the eco-checklist, designed by Richard.

An Inconvenient Tour Buffalo Gals Road Trip 2007
Ten things to do
. . . one van at a time
Check your tires
Turn off your lights
Lower your thermostat
Abandon your homes
Carpool with ten others
Bear Witness
Write a Haiku
Bark for Treats
Explore Beef Jerky as an alternative fuel
Control your greenhouse gases . . .

TOUR 2007

Holy-moly in Big Valley, Alberta.

PHOTO: BOB ERKAMP

TWENTY

AN INCONVENIENT TOUR

PRESENT:

All

Friday, June 8, 2007

The Edmonton folks arrive in Red Deer a little bit early for the nine o'clock rendezvous, so I bully the lads (Robert, Richard, Tyler, and Stephen) into a stop at the Francis the Pig statue. (I want to know the name of the artist.) The van drops me in front of the pig. There's a group of well-dressed men sitting on the bench behind Francis, so I feel a need to explain why I'm crouching down in front of the pig with a notebook. The three of them all have very witty suggestions about the name of the pig sculptor. When I get back into the van—which is slowly creeping away pretending to leave me behind—oh funny ha ha—my companions have already decided that this little side street must be Red Deer's gay village. As we park the van and walk around this area of downtown, more evidence to support this

205

theory presents itself. (Who knew there was an alternative community in Red Deer?)

We meet at the Velvet Olive (first enjoyed during Tour 2003) for a martini and the first of our loud and convivial get-togethers. Happily there's a separate room in the back where our hooting and hollering is not quite as conspicuous, but the clientele definitely thins out after our arrival. (A new business idea: need a room cleared, hire the Gals!)

The drinks are flowing and we're delighted to discover that "Suzie," the owner/operater, can feed us too! She has both steaks and burgers on offer—our kind of gal—which she cooks on the barbecue just outside the door to the bar. Once you get your piece of perfectly grilled meat, you make your way to a little buffet set up at the other end of the bar to load up on pasta salad, bread and condiments. Splendid. It's even faintly reminiscent of the cook-your-own-steak bar in Patricia.

It must also be noted that this is, bar none, the most economical meal the Gals have ever had. The burgers and steaks (with fixins') are under ten dollars, and the drinks are more than fairly priced as well. It's never been our objective to cheap out on the food and beverages, but we can't help but be pleased at the final tally. And after plenty of guffawing, hooting, and hollering up and down the table, complemented by red wine and martinis, we've successfully completed Stage One: Real Life Debrief and Initial Whoop-up. We're so pleased we decide to come back here for breakfast . . .

After a night at the Travelodge, we do just that. The other side of the Velvet Olive, once you follow through from its back alley location to Ross Street, is "Café Pichilingue." We straggle in the next morning for terrific "Hot Bitch Wake the Fuck Up" blend coffee (that's really the name, I swear), French toast with cream cheese and strawberries, and Mexican sausages. Again—a most economical, delicious, and cheerful repast.

Red Deer grows in my estimation every time the Gals come through for a feed and a hotel bed. Having grown up in this neck of the woods and gone to college here for a year, Red Deer has always been firmly placed in my mind as an ultra-conservative (and dull) little city of mini-malls and half-tons. But there's a lot of interesting stuff going on here—the arts scene is thriving—the population is more diverse and interesting than ever before. And hey—if you can feed and water the discerning (okay, gluttonous) Gals several times over and send them away without a whimper, that must speak to the city's restaurant scene.

That said, we're soon to be deep into "Cross and Bones" country. This phrase, coined by the director (Paul Carriere) of the documentary *The Cross and Bones*, refers to the fact that the Tyrrell Museum of Paleontology exists cheek by jowl with the creationist Christians in the area. The documentary includes a scene between the guy who plays Jesus in the Drumheller Passion Play (who also happens to be a realtor) and one of the chief paleontologists at the Tyrell (who happens to be listing his house). What a truly comical encounter.

Anyway, this is a most interesting corridor of the province, rich with dinosaur bones, fundamentalist beliefs, dead beautiful scenery, and conflicting points of view. The Creation "Science" Museum is right in the zone.

We pile into the van and head east from Red Deer.

The Creation Museum is a little one-floor building with a big model out front of a child playing with a dinosaur. Once you step inside, you're transported into another world, premised on the following notions:

1. The earth is less than ten thousand years old.

2. Fossils aren't really all that hard to create, and thus aren't really proof of anything. (The museum displays a "fossilized" teddy bear and cowboy boot.)

3. Dinosaurs and humans roamed the earth together until they were wiped out by the Great Flood. (As in Noah's ark. The museum also claims that the ark has been sighted several times since 1959.)

4. The genealogy of King Henry VI traces back to Adam and Eve. Well for that matter, Princes William and Harry can be traced to Adam and Eve, too!

And so on.

I'm standing at the very first display when a man wearing a John Deere cap and fierce expression sidles up beside me. Says "this is something, huh?" That much I can agree with, so I nod and murmur "uh-huh." He catches my eye, says in a passionate undertone, "and when you think of the lies they're teaching our kids in school . . ." He trails off, indignant, no doubt waiting for a sympathetic rejoinder. I really don't want to engage in this argument, so I just turn back to the display. He moves on after a moment, perhaps to find another true believer in the crowd. Poor fellow—the museum is full of Buffalo Gals ogling the displays with open-mouthed astonishment. I sidle up beside Patti two or three times; we make faces at each other in response to the displays. Kevin's over by one of nouveau fossils making appalled, clucking noises. Robert moves slowly from panel to panel, his brow furrowed. I squeeze his hand—his scientific mind is clearly reeling.

There's a whole bit about engravings on a tomb from 1496, depicting animals which the creationists claim look like dinosaurs. In other words dinosaurs and humans co-existed as recently as 1496. Jeez, you'd think there'd be some mention of this in writings from this time period. Like, "Me Mum was roasting a fine fowl over the fire when twas untimely snatched and devoured by young Finnigan's tyrannosaurus." But nope—it's the best-kept secret of the fifteenth century.

A quote from the museum's website claims: "I spent more time in this museum than I did in the Smithsonian." We, however, follow our usual, well-established patterns. Both Robert and Bob disappear early on. (Bob reads something about dinosaur tracks heading in the same direction as those of creatures fleeing the biblical Flood; that does him in.) Norma, on the other hand, reads every single panel in the place.

I must confess I don't hang in there for the duration, so perhaps I'm not a proper judge of the contents. I do notice a disturbing trend, however, in the material I plough through. When in doubt, the author often makes the claim that the natural element in question is just too complicated to have "evolved" on its own; thus there must have been a "master designer." Over and over again this is used as the clincher in the argument.

Finally it's time to take our leave and to encounter owner operator Harry Niburg who is manning the guest book. I decide to take my cue from Stephen, who is bemused but polite when Harry solicits feedback. Stephen simply says something about "fascinating points of view," and makes an exit. Meanwhile Tyler is hovering over the book display and I'm afraid there might be a scene. (Tyler has a devout passion for literature and treasures books above all other earthly possessions.) He picks up a few of the brightly-coloured children's books (*The Beginning of All Things*) and sets them down again, as if contemplating a hurl across the room.

We're all inspired to document our impressions in the scrapbook . . .

> *Global Flood Threatens*
> *Dinosaurs Run Away Fast*
> *Fuck Evolution*
>
> *Dinosaurs Grazing*
> *Storm Clouds on the Horizon*
> *Noah, worried, sighs.*
>
> *Tyler was an ape?*
> *Fossils form faster these days*
> *He is old monkey*

There's nothing better to take the edge off an experience like this than cinnamon buns. Our host at the Creation Museum, Harry, phones ahead to find out when the buns will be coming out of the oven at the café over in the nearby boardwalk area we visited in 2002. (I think this is terribly Albertan of him: "We may disagree but I'd never see you go hungry.") As we wait for our sticky treats, and for Norma, we're mightily amused to discover a huge pool full of frogs (for sale) in one of the stores close to the cinnamon bun café.

One last item on the agenda. Somehow we have to get a group shot of ourselves in front of the Creation Museum without engaging anyone in conversation about Darwin. We quickly huddle around the sign in our conspicuous lime-green T-shirts and position ourselves so that the dinosaur-frolicking-with-little-girl is in the shot.

Back in the van, Stephen shares a quote from the play he's just finished directing.

"Rock me—rock my chicken." Don't ask me what the context is for this line of dialogue, but it's definitely noted in the scrapbook, and is instantly integrated into our van talk. Now we hit the road to hunt down the literary component of our trip, sadly lacking in previous years—and perhaps sadly lacking in the above quote from Stephen.

Stephan G. Stephansson was born in Iceland in 1853. He emigrated, ending up in Markerville, Alberta, where he lived until his death in 1927. Often called the "greatest poet of the western world," he was also incredibly prolific, publishing more than two thousand pages of poetry during his seventy-three years. This is all the more remarkable given the circumstances under which he wrote: he worked as a farmer from dawn till dusk, often composing poems while haying or milking the cows. As if this wasn't enough to occupy his time, Stephansson was also a noted pacifist, boldly speaking out against war in the early part of the last century.

From the Alberta Online Encyclopedia, and the Heritage Community Foundation:

"Essentially a man of the nineteenth century, he believed in the power of words. A true romantic, he was sure that ideas and ideals, given the wings of verse, could overcome the problems of the human race."

I can't decide whether or not I find that depressing or inspiring. Let's just say it's a challenging and worthwhile notion. But certainly Stephansson's legacy lives on. His poetry, credited with rejuvenating the Icelandic language, is still studied in schools there. Here in Canada his poetic soul survives in the person of his great-grandson Bill Bourne, a fabulous Alberta musician with a gift for stirring poetic lyrics, and one of the most distinctive singing voices in the business.

Stephansson's farm is way off the beaten track, on Highway 592. The charming wooden house, painted the colour of Pepto-Bismol, sits atop a gentle rise. I'm sure the view from the veranda inspired many a poetic thought. We don't tarry for long, however, as the mosquitoes are the size of sparrows and we're being harried and nipped at every step. Oh, and Bob is agitating for ice cream . . .

Markerville is a tiny little hamlet built alongside the Medicine River. The historic Markerville Creamery, no longer operative, has a craft shop and a café serving ice cream. We all have a cone and wander across the bridge and back. Tyler lobbies hard for our group to visit the Markerville Boy Scout Museum. The "museum" looks to be a labour of love, as it's housed in a tiny, private home sporting a somewhat makeshift sign. Tyler's pleas fall on deaf ears.

Besides, as Bob keeps reminding us about every twenty minutes, "we have to be at Goldeye by seven." (That's a scheduled MEAL he's referring to.) Of course he also frequently says, "If I didn't love ya, I'd hate ya." Both phrases are strong inducements to get the hell back in the van.

We pick up Highway 11 west of Sylvan Lake and make good time to Rocky Mountain House, where we fill up on gas and buy bags of cherries for munching in the van. Proceeding toward Nordegg on the David Thompson Highway, we're heading deeper and deeper into the wilds. The Rocky Mountains are looming and so is our dinner.

The Goldeye Centre, a beautiful log complex, is perched prettily above Goldeye Lake, just a few minutes west of Nordegg. We're due for dinner there by no later than 7 PM; we make it with a half-hour to spare. We're booked into the "Church Hoppins Wing," named after a couple of the founding fathers. There's just enough time before dinner for our orientation session—including warnings about cougars and bears—with one of the extremely cheerful Goldeye staff members.

Dinner! There are pork chops and gravy and plenty of spuds! And Caesar salad and green beans and desserts—we feel like we've just been to Mom's house for supper. The food is plentiful and delicious, and except for another group who stay mysteriously sequestered in their own quarters, we seem to be the only ones on site to enjoy it. At some point during dinner the question arises—there's a murder of crows, a gaggle of geese. What do you call a bunch of buffalo? The winning entry is submitted by Richard: we're a JERKY. A jerky of buffalo! Splendid.

Now we're in for one of those "ain't much to do" evenings. A few of us go to Nordegg to buy provisions (wine and beer) while the rest of the crew naps and/or gets a fire started in our lodge. For the princely sum of one dollar a head, the Goldeye folks have provided us with a bucket of salty treats, pop, and marshmallows to roast over the fire. What follows is one of the most pleasant times we've ever spent together.

Patti and Richard, both inveterate poker players, set up a card game and offer to tutor the neophyte—me. Along with Robert and Kevin, we play for hours. It's fantastic, addictive fun. Meanwhile, over on the couch, Stephen, Brian, and Norma toss back white wine and have a long, philosophical discussion about the state of theatre and drama education and lord knows what else. I occasionally tune in for a little taste of erudition to cut the grease of my lowbrow poker fun. But really, the card game takes every ounce of my concentration, and even then I often have to ask Patti to advise me on my hand.

I suppose we're lucky Stephen hasn't taken this notion of the camp-fire too much to heart cause lemme tell ya, if you ever wanna sing a campfire song—and WHY WOULDN'T YOU?! Anyway, if you ever wanna sing a camp song—and by that I mean a big, cheerful, lung-bustin' tune typically sung by children around a fire, not some coyly warbled Noel Coward number. Okay, like, returning to my point, if you ever want to sing a camp song, Stephen KNOWS THEM ALL. He has a lovely tenor voice and a memory like some kind of deranged pachyderm. And if you get him wound up on this topic, he'll just sing and sing and sing. Rooms will clear out, birthdays will pass, stars may fade from our hemisphere, and the only two people left singing "Oh they built the Ship Titanic to sail the ocean blue . . ." will be me and Stephen. (And I'll be holding the songbook cause I can't remember the lyrics.)

Tyler is stretched out on the couch reading the latest piece of great literature. (Tyler always has a couple of great paperbacks in his knapsack, and he's never even slightly judgemental when he recommends you read the latest Michael Ondaatje instead of the *People* magazine or trashy potboiler you brought along for the trip. At bedtime, when I complain that I've forgotten to bring reading material, he hands over a crisp new copy of Jeanette Walls's fabulous memoir *The Glass Castle*. He hasn't even cracked the book himself and he's giving it to me!) And Bob seems to be mostly content staring into the fire, reading magazines, and occasionally weighing in on other people's conversations.

The mountain air that spills in through our bedroom windows that night is bristly cold and smells of pine trees. We sleep like the dead.

Happy to have survived our wilderness adventure at Goldeye Centre.
PHOTO: PATTI PON

After a jolly, generous breakfast, a shopping frenzy in the gift shop, and many, many photos in front of the main lodge and the giant dinner bell, we're off. West on Highway 11, heading toward Jasper National Park. Did I mention that Richard has been driving this entire trip?? Some kind of kooky deal with the insurance company. Apparently it was more costly to ensure more than one driver; actually none of us were really clear on the deal until it was too late to change the rental agreement. So. Richard spends virtually this entire trip behind the wheel. (We cheat on the last leg of the journey and Bob drives us home.)

That said, there are folks in the van who like to drive and those who don't. Richard and Robert both love to drive—and drive and drive. This is partly a control issue, and partly a social one. The hours of wisecracking badinage in the van can get a little intense, like being force-fed six or seven pieces of delicious cheesecake instead of the one and a half you really wanted. Escaping to the driver's seat is a great way to get out of the line of fire. Plus, the Gals aren't stingy with their approval for tricky van maneuvers. Execute a particularly difficult left turn and the whole group does a thunderously loud, staccato-rhythmic spate of applause. We do a LOT of clapping in the van.

Control is another matter. The driver gets to pick the tunes on the CD player, the driver gets to hoard snacks at the front of the van, the driver can make unscheduled stops.

Sunday, after breakfast, Richard makes just such a stop at Crescent Falls, a few minutes off Highway 11. It's lovely—and we're falling further and further behind schedule.

We pee (and get coffee) at Saskatchewan River Crossing, then turn onto Highway 93 to head toward the icefields. And soon experience one of the highlights of the trip . . .

Wow-wow-wow . . . not one but TWO bears! They're grazing right beside the highway. We slow down—we'd be pretty much forced to even if we didn't want to, cause there are at least fifteen vehicles parked on either side of the road. Most people sit in their cars, or hang out the windows, rapt at the scene. A few dunderheads have edged into the little meadow, just metres away from the bears. The bears—a mother and child—completely ignore all of us.

> *Grizzly bear sighting*
> *Japanese make great sushi*
> *I mean for the bears*

> *Grizzly bear sighting*
> *Stupid tourists approach them*
> *Darwin had it right*

Upon sober second thought we realize that these are probably brown bears, not grizzlies as we first thought. But, still! We're all tickled absolutely pink to catch a glimpse of these creatures.

It's good to be reminded of what a stunning gift this landscape and wildlife represents, because it's easy to get blasé about our mountain parks. Shocking, huh? Tourists come from all over the world to catch a glimpse of the Rocky Mountains, or of bears and sheep and goats. And we Albertans almost take this majesty for granted.

Many of us Gals have spent substantial stretches of time working at the Banff Centre for the Arts, where encountering rutting elks on your way back from the bar is almost commonplace. There's a joke in there somewhere, but I am trying desperately to take the high road . . .

Speaking of high roads.

From the Jasper National Park website:

The Columbia Icefield is a surviving remnant of the thick ice mass that once mantled most of Western Canada's mountains. Lying on a wide, elevated plateau, it is the largest icefield in the Canadian Rockies. The Athabasca is the most-visited glacier on the North American continent. Its ice is in continuous motion, creeping forward at the rate of several centimeters per day. Spilling from the Columbia Icefield over three giant bedrock steps, the glacier flows down the valley like a frozen, slow-moving river. Because of a warming climate, the Athabasca Glacier has been receding or melting for the last 125 years. Losing half its volume and retreating more than 1.5 kilometres, the shrinking glacier has left a moonscape of rocky moraines in its wake.

Over half of the Gals have been to the Columbia Icefields at some point in their lives. As the site comes into view, some of the long-time Albertans reflect on how much the glacier has receded since their first childhood visit. (A LOT.) Almost as shocking is the wholesale development of this site by Brewster and Co. The parking lot is full to bursting. The Columbia Icefield Centre, teeming with tourists from every corner of the globe, houses an Interpretive Centre/Museum, a couple of restaurants, and a gift shop. It also serves as the leaping off point for the tours of the glacier. It's a little bit like visiting an airport. It's all a bit creepy.

Although really, what in the world did we expect? And how else would you accommodate the thousands of visitors who are interested in seeing something move at a glacial pace? That said, we do wonder if any of the gazillions of dollars made at this extremely popular tourist attraction are funnelled back into the park or used to preserve the site. Maybe we're just acting out our own guilt for flocking to the glacier to pick over the remains of the last ice age. We ain't part of the solution, that's for sure. We pay our thirty-five bucks, have a sandwich and wait for the tour to begin.

A bus takes us across the highway and to the edge of the glacier where we board a "Snocoach." These enormous all-terrain vehicles can schlep about fifty people a couple of kilometres up to a thrilling vantage point at about seventy-five hundred feet high: a giant meadow of old ice formed from snow falling as long as four hundred years ago.

There's time for photos and frolic, you can even dip a cup into a stream of ice blue melted-glacier water and have a sip. Up here on the continental divide, we really do feel like we're at the top of the world. It's nearly 4 PM when we finally stumble back to the van. It's starting to dawn on the Edmonton folks that we still have a coupla items on the agenda before we start the long drive back north.

We retrace our route down the ice valley parkway. We see the bears again, in exactly the same place, placidly munching the grass by the highway. We're delighted to catch another glimpse of our friends, but a little astounded (alarmed) that they're still in place. Could they be animatronics? Or just heavily sedated?

Our settling-up dinner in Canmore is our only expensive meal of the trip, and possibly the least satisfying. Richard is so tired he can hardly lift his fork; he looks like he's been dragged behind the van for a day or two. The spinach salad is disappointing, and there's a teensy bit of tension about the final stage of the travel arrangements. The Edmontonians are desperate for one of the Calgarians to take Stephen and Tyler to the airport so we can take a more direct route home. The Calgarians aren't thrilled about missing the final episode of *The Sopranos*.

I think it's the most testiness we've ever had at any point of any of our trips. (And really, it was no big whoop.) We're just a bunch of very tired children who've spent a little too long at an amusement park. I'm reminded, once again, of what a great deal of personality there is in that little van. And why maybe we're destined never to take the fifteen day all-around-the-world marathon trip that Tyler keeps promoting as a tenth anniversary option . . .

On June 11 07 at 12:49 Richard wrote:
Thanks to all who participated in another wonderful weekend. On the way back we were discussing distances, and I think this year we may have set a record. Conni thought the previous record was 1200 kilometres. I am pleased to announce that this year we managed to do 1443 kilometres!

Gas total after final fill-up came to $155 so I will set aside the extra $20 to invest in GICs for next year. I had a lovely time!

Richard

On June 12 7:50 AM Stephen wrote:
Thanks to you for all the driving. Next year we cough up extra bucks so that we can share the joy at the wheel.

And a new record, huh? It still felt like that first year we put on more clicks than you could shake a proverbial marshmallow stick at.

You guys are all mega-fun to travel with. I will dine out on the Creation Science Museum for a long time!

Till we meet again—soon, I hope.

xxxxxxxxxxxxxxxxxxxxxxStephen

On June 12 10:30 AM Bob wrote:
And ditto from me and Kevin too!!!!

On June 12 1 PM Conni wrote:
It was perfectly grand! We saw bears! Two of them—twice! I loved our gentle hoe-down on Saturday night and the weighty conclusions drawn about weed whackers and biblical knowledge—HA! Smooches to you all! Conni and Robert

On June 12 1:30 PM Tyler wrote:
Thank you Richard for all your pedal to the metal. You really do deserve a medal. The 1443 kilometres that the Buffalo Gals travelled this year is only 21 kilometres short of a one-way trip between Edmonton and Yellowknife according to the United Van Lines website. That's a lot of highway.

Thanks to everyone for making this a fabulous way to conclude our holiday. It was a pleasure to see Conni blossom into the Poker (you brought 'er) Queen that she has become. Move over Tina Wallman!

The crumbling Icefields reminded me of what it means to be a cold Canadian.

Thanks again for a fantastic weekend.

I look forward to our tenth anniversary!!

A sign seen on the "inconvenient tour," sometime late Sunday afternoon:

FREE THE WEST!

Something else to put on the Buffalo Gals agenda . . .

Columbia Icefields.
PHOTO: BOB ERKAMP

TOUR 2008

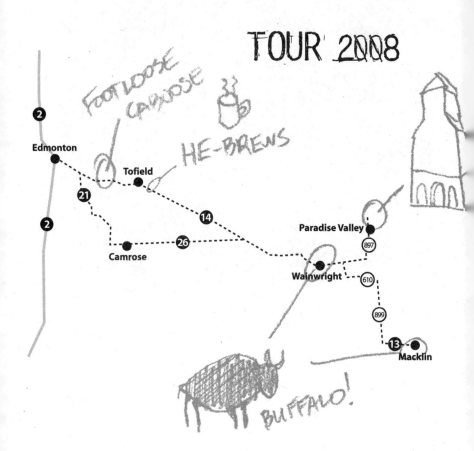

FOOTLOOSE CABOOSE

HE-BREWS

2 Edmonton

21

2

Tofield

14

26

Camrose

Paradise Valley

897

Wainwright

610

899

13 Macklin

BUFFALO!

Definitely not a household pet.
PHOTO: NORMA LOCK

TWENTY-ONE

A JERKY OF BUFFALO

"Van on the prairies
A decade of buffalo
Just so much jerky"
—one of Stephen's haiku from the scrapbook
PS: Haiku are sposed to feature an element of nature, not
just food and stuff.
      —an anonymous editorial comment scrawled
                  on the last page of this year's scrapbook

There is a LOT of discussion about what to do to commemorate ten years of Buffalo Gals. Should we try to get a corporate jet to fly us to our top ten locations from the last ten years? Patti knows someone who knows someone who rents out rock star buses—complete with wet bar, biffy and bunks—we could just park it in the middle of a canola field and party down. Or should we bust out of the provincial boundaries and head for the Kootenays—or east to Moose Jaw?

221

Heavens forfend! The Gals have vowed never to road trip outside Alberta.

But sometimes the most obvious choice is the best one. During the early winter of 2008, Robert and I see a little article in the AMA magazine about a company dedicated to BUFFALO ADVENTURES in Wainwright, Alberta. What are we about, if not "buffalo adventures"? What are we if not Buffalo Adventurers? What could be more perfect—and yes, more obvious—than communing with our namesakes in the animal kingdom?

I start the campaign in early winter, sending out the link to the website, placing the appropriate amount of emphasis on the comestibles. When I do my PowerPoint presentation at the planning brunch in March, I pitch strategically, dropping my speech (with handouts) into that lull between ordering food and getting food, but timing it carefully so that blood sugar levels are not yet dangerously low.

After I've finished my dog and pony show, the Gals exhibit the gentle enthusiasm we're known for. (White cowboy hats flung in the air, restaurant tables overturned.) No—lest we sound undiscerning— I could say that everyone promised to peruse the links to the website and get back to me at some later date. Nah . . . it was an easy sell. It was, afterall, our year to head in a northerly direction, (Wainwright is about three hours east of Edmonton), and there were other powerful deciding factors as well.

1. The AMA magazine article promoting the tours features a photo of Kevin's aunt and uncle, by some wild coincidence. Now that's just spooky—must be a sign!

2. Norma has always, always wanted a buffalo rug.

3. I refer you to the list of tours offered by Buffalo Adventures and invite you to draw some conclusions of your own.

From the website:

"Parks and POWs"—tour the former Buffalo National Park and the German officer Prisoner of War camp in Wainwright, now operating as one of Canada's most advanced military training bases. A herd of buffalo at the entry gate reflects the origins of the base, the former Buffalo National Park.

"Dig in at Bodo"—uncover the true Aboriginal culture of the plains at one of the richest archeological dig sites in western Canada.

"Buffalo Past and Present"—examine an operating plains buffalo ranch, find out how today's buffalo wranglers go about their work, see buffalo up close, and learn about their history and habitat from experts in the field. Also sample bison cuisine and see some leather products.

Stop right there. Perhaps you know us well enough by now to understand that we had no need to look further than "bison cuisine" (grub!) and "leather products" (retail!). The Gals were "in."

I should say there are a number of other adventures on offer from this great young company. I think I can speak for all of the Gals when I say I have no doubt that there's wisdom aplenty to be gained by visiting the Wainwright railway interpretative park or by touring Alberta's largest neo-Gothic church. (Please believe me that I am utterly sincere when I say that.) That said, I'm thinkin' the Gals don't need to learn about rotational grazing. And maybe we're not so keen on a "visit to a working feedlot." For better or worse, we have chosen our path. We will head east from Edmonton toward Wainwright and see what kind of trouble we can get into . . .

I begin a correspondence with the lovely Jennifer Ford of Buffalo Adventures. The Buffalo Gals have never bought a package deal before, unless you count Patti's friend Leonard giving us a tour of Red Deer in year one, complete with Timbits. Jennifer's offer to plan a whole twenty-four hours of our forty-eight is mighty appealing, and may possibly cut down on the amount of time we spend driving around in circles in the van looking for beef dip.

On May 22, Jennifer finalized our itinerary. Yippee-whah-hoo.

Dear Conni,

Your adventure will begin at 10:30 AM at the Old Wainwright Train

Station, where you will pick up interpretive maps and information for the next leg of your Adventure. Directions to the Wainwright Train Station have been provided below.

After you pick up your orientation packet, you will drive approximately 1 hour and 15 minutes through our beautiful parkland to east of Provost, Alberta. Here you will experience our Buffalo Past and Present Adventure. First you will enjoy a lunch featuring some of our local buffalo cuisine and good western hospitality. Then you will tour this modern bison ranch, see their plains bison herd, learn about modern ranching methods, and the history of your farm family hosts, Bob, Carl, and Irma Rehman.

Your adventure will last three hours. This Adventure is outdoors. Typically we are lucky to boast nice weather in this part of Alberta, but the weather here can also change quickly. Please come prepared with light rain gear and good footwear as you may do some walking or climbing. Make sure you bring your camera! There are many opportunities to take some outstanding shots of the bison. There are also homemade bison products including moccasins, leather gloves, and bison meat that can be purchased on this site with cash or cheque.

Following your Adventure, you will make your way back to Wainwright. You can settle in to the R&R Inn where suites have been set aside for you under the name Buffalo Adventures. Supper will be provided for you at the Honey Pot Eatery and Pub, an award-winning local eating establishment that boasts a variety of local fare.

Please note: alcoholic beverages are not covered in the price of this package.

On Sunday morning, breakfast will be provided for you at the Galleria Restaurant located in the Old Train Station.

Attached, please find our Buffalo Adventures waivers, which need to be signed by you and the members of your group.

We look forward to hosting you in east-central Alberta.

Of course absolutely nothing on this itinerary went according to plan—except for the western hospitality. But I have to admit that signing a waiver (for the first time ever) got us thinking . . . what kind of waiver would you design for a Buffalo Gals tour, if some unsuspecting soul were attending for the very first time?

Caution: Van may contain nuts.

Or, perhaps more practically addressing potential safety issues:

Participants are asked to keep arms and legs and other body parts inside the van while it is moving. Especially the other body parts. If participants return home with fewer body parts than when commencing the journey, they probably have only themselves to blame. Which is sort of a central Albertan way of saying: we're not liable for your stupidity. You got pie-eyed at the tavern and you wanna sue the owner cause you totalled your truck on the way home? As if. So you lost a finger in the combine, that's just the way she goes. Is John Deere your babysitter or something? No sir.

Or, perhaps put more simply:

We ain't responsible for you having a good time or a bad time. That's all on you, honey . . .

TWENTY-TWO

A DECA-DENCE OF BUFFALO

PRESENT:
all but Kevin
ABSENT:
Kevin

Hang on . . .

June 7, 2008: Less than one week before the road trip and we still don't have a plan for Friday night dinner. (It must be said that, while we're all delighted to have survived and thrived for ten years as an entity, the pressure to come up with novel dining and sight-seeing concepts grows apace.) In a perfect world, there'd be some sort of fine dining establishment outside Edmonton, conveniently located enroute to Wainwright. In an even more perfect world, this dining establishment would not only have a wine list, it would have some sort of character. The hours and days tick by—will we Edmontonians have to present some kind of dinner theatre in the van—sandwiches in a hamper along with skits—in lieu of a real Buffalo Gals grub fest? Tuesday night—three days before our Friday departure—Brian's good friend Frannie, who lives out by Tofield (see map), comes to the rescue with a suggestion for a dining establishment that might meet all our requirements.

Sometimes this really is a perfect world.

Friday, June 13

The Buffalo Gals convene their tenth annual road trip at approximately 6:07 PM at the home of Robert and Conni. Members drink margaritas, nibble on vegetables and Mundare sausage, debrief the week previous, wind up the banter for the weekend ahead, process fifteen to twenty bathroom breaks (some of them pre-emptive strikes?), pack and repack the van. Hit the road @ 7:18.

We have a crisis of faith about forty minutes outside of Edmonton. We're headed for a restaurant called the "Footloose Caboose," but somehow, after following the directions to the letter, we have ended up on a country road in the middle of nowhere. It seems unlikely that there would be a restaurant anywhere in this neck of the woods. Then we see a little red caboose on a post: the mailbox marking the driveway to our destination.

We drive into the yard; everywhere we look, there are train cars! Our spirits soar. Which is to say, one person after another tumbles out of the van sporting a mile-wide grin. Tyler leaps out of the front seat where he's been riding shotgun and runs around in an excited little circle like a high-strung Labrador puppy. Norma beams at the photo ops. Certainly we were expecting the caboose theme suggested by the name of the restaurant to be carried through in the décor, but this is way, way over the top. In a good way.

According to Eva Loranger, co-owner of Footloose Caboose, this all started with a glimpse of a broken-down train car in a lot at the edge of the city. Eva knows her trains—LOVES her trains—and she saw potential where others might have seen rust heap. Closer examination revealed the remains of a Mount Lefroy observation car, built in 1909 by the Canadian Pacific Railway. Eva and her husband Ray bought the car for a song and spent several years refurbishing it after hauling it out to their little farm. Now it's the Footloose Caboose, fitted out with linen and china, and looking at least as elegant as it must have been in its original incarnation.

It sits in the middle of a farmyard, across the way from a completely restored caboose containing a bed and a hot tub. (Now there are two of these cabooses, suitable for guest bookings.) Right beside the caboose: a restored Grand Trunk Pacific train station (residence of the owners). And—wait for it—a barbed wire museum. I am so purely, completely, utterly delighted by this latter discovery that I'm pretty much speechless. But there'll be time later to explore. We climb up the stairs into the dining car . . .

The menu looks great, with Eva's Czech heritage reflected in the chicken paprika and the fabulous dessert selection. After we've ordered drinks, it's time for the traditional unveiling of the T-shirts.

Richard has outdone himself on the occasion of our tenth anniversary. The graphic is an homage to that beautiful image from Head-Smashed-In Buffalo Jump: noble creatures leaping from right nipple to left, with the necessary and unique addition of a white van in the middle of the herd. This year's tour title: "Head Smashed in Buffalo Gals." Possibly the best T-shirt so far! We proudly don our uniforms, and wait for the first course . . .

Dinner is outstanding, particularly the cauliflower soup, sweet and sour sauerkraut, and poached pears. We love our charming host, and are a little bit in awe of the fact that all this food comes out of a tiny galley kitchen at the other end of the car, complete with grandchildren underfoot. One gets a glimpse of that little dream factory along a narrow passage on the way to the bathroom. If there's a lineup for the biffy, one can always peruse the selection of crafts for sale, displayed on a tall, narrow shelf, OR pick out your favourite kind of barbed wire from a poster mounted on the wall. (The museum's outside, but this is a teaser.)

The barbed wire poster provides a totally unexpected word feast, a lip-smacking poetical buffet, as the names for the different designs are evocative, quirky, and weirdly appropriate for each different variation on the barbed wire theme. (e.g., Elwood Kink, Decker Spread, Crandel Champion, Allis Buckthorn.) We instantly adopt the barbed wire monikers as character names—I clamour to be the hopelessly elegant "Glidden Twist"—and we all begin to riff on the plot of a murder mystery starring these exotic folks, entitled either *The Mont Lefroy Murders* or *The Devil's Rope*. (The latter being a nickname for barbed wire.) The plot outline of said bestseller was transcribed by Patti onto a paper napkin—damned if any of it makes sense now.

Speaking of characters, the human drama unspools around us all during dinner. Just as we're getting our first round of drinks, a young couple with a baby have words. They tumble out into the yard outside the train car, seemingly just on the verge of physical violence. The guy (daddy?), with a baby's milk bottle crammed in the back pocket of his tight jeans, grabs the woman's arm—she pulls away. One more time. We can hear them shouting. A couple of staff members hold watch at a train window, ready to intervene if things get ugly . . . ?

One of the observers is a gent wearing a worn plaid mackinaw, a forbidding expression, and dark caterpillar fringes above his snappy brown eyes. His appearance, and the fact that he's reprimanding one of the kids "helping out" (getting underfoot), add up to the overall impression of a stern authority figure. We think we've got him pegged and then, in the pleasant chatty aftermath of dinner, we're introduced to him as Ray, Eva's husband and our co-host. Ray, it turns out, is a witty and articulate raconteur. He provides the single most important piece of trivia we've ever encountered on these trips: the real story behind our anthem, "Buffalo Gals." According to Ray, the "gals" referred to in this song were actually prostitutes, trolling for prospects during the construction of the Erie Canal. And that iconic line, "Buffalo gals, won't you come out tonight?" just takes on a whole different flavour, huh?

We pay up, buy some crafts, then wander around the farmyard. At one end of the yard there are tall racks displaying telephone insulators. These beautiful pieces of glass, which come in a variety of shapes and a rainbow of colours, are backlit by the setting sun. Looking beyond them, out into a field, we see some miscellaneous farm equipment, and more cabooses awaiting restoration. (They're up to seven now.) Before we leave, we must of course gather around the display of barbed wire samples + signage that constitutes the "museum." We scribble down a few more barbed wire names in the scrapbook, enjoy an extended farewell scene with Eva and Ray, and head toward our accommodations in the big old town of Tofield . . .

After checking in at our hotel we go to the Last Chance Saloon and encounter the usual looks from the locals when we pile out of the white van. (What do we look like, I wonder? Hipsters? Dorks? Ghostbusters?) We order up a round of drinks. The bartender/waitress looks a little shell-shocked, says this is the most people she's ever had in the bar at one time. The locals are friendly enough, but devoid of curiosity about what the hell we're doing here. We're mighty curious about them—especially the two young men sporting gi-normous mohawks (no, really, like an eighteen-inch sculpted razor edge atop their heads), the requisite piercings, and . . . white cotton pants. Huh?

Robert and I oversleep the next morning. (The alarm never went off, I swear.) When we finally tumble out of our room at the Beaverhill Motel, the entire crew is ranged around the van, WAITING. A mere twenty minute delay inspires nearly two pages of ill-tempered haiku in the scrapbook.

We buy snacks at the Tofield IGA where I engage a local woman in conversation—where can we get some coffee? (Perhaps I'll be forgiven for delaying the proceedings this morning if I'm able to address this urgent need.) The woman confers with her friend. "Well there's the Husky station one block over, of course." I try not to grimace as I imagine how the gas station sludge will go over with this crowd. "Or . . . ," she continues uncertainly, "they serve coffee at the church." She and her friend confer about whether or not said coffee place will actually be open today. I'm sufficiently intrigued to get directions. I know this is going to involve a little sell job back in the van. As you may recall, organized religion does from time to time, er, um, inspire diverse and powerful reactions in this crowd . . .

Once we find the Tofield Gospel Church, Bob and Norma decline to leave the van. The rest of us go in to do a little reconnaissance.

The coffee shop, rather wittily named "He-brews," has a fully kitted-out expresso machine; every fancy-arse coffee you might want is on offer, including mochachinos, cappucinos and americanos. I try to sniff out the religious propaganda as the friendly (bible-toting??) barrista starts to work on our orders. Ah-ha! There ain't no grande lattes here, no—the Lord's morning ambrosia is served in three sizes: David (small), Joshua (medium), and—you guessed it—Goliath! Forty minutes later we're on the road again, impressed with our coffee and the brilliant soul-gathering strategy employed by the church.

We drive by the small town of Viking, home to the famous Sutter hockey dynasty of six stick-handling brothers. Six, count them, SIX boys to take to early morning practices and drive to tournaments all over the countryside. Doesn't it make you want to meet the Sutter parents? We briefly consider tracking them down, but our destiny awaits in Wainwright.

As I mentioned, the whole Wainwright itinerary had already gone through a few revisions with the patient accommodation of Jennifer. (What with our morning tardiness and all, it was deemed more reasonable to start the tour a little later and bump our buffalo/bison meal to the evening.) But no one had accounted for the unseasonably wet weather . . .

We arrive at the Wainwright train station, pick up tour packages, meet Jennifer, and have lunch. (A couple of the Gals actually order bison burgers—sheesh!) Jennifer proposes another change in plan due to the rain: she's worried we'll get stuck in a field if we travel in our van. So she's arranged for two 4X4 vehicles to transport us to the bison ranch. Brian, Robert, Stephen, and I end up in a big SUV piloted by Jennifer's father. And thus begins the value-added portion of the tour . . .

The genial Mr. Brower is a veritable font of information about absolutely everything we see outside the window of the truck: the wildlife, the crops, the trees, the bison, the military base. We are all saddened to hear that none of his children have immediate plans to take over the farm that's been in his family for a couple of generations. (Really, it doesn't sound financially feasible for them to do so.)

However, since daughter Jennifer is married to a farmer (the handsome young beekeeper driving the other vehicle), perhaps they'll buy the family land someday.

Most importantly, we're starting to have a very special experience we're going to enjoy for the rest of the day. Feeling a little tiny bit like aliens. (In a good way.) You know when you tumble off the midnight train in Istanbul, or gather in a cluster to hear the translator describe how the locals dye carpets, or make pottery, or train fighting cocks? Mr. Brower is a down-home guy who's giving us a lift to a ranch; he's also our tour guide, and as such is talking to us like we're from Latvia or New Jersey or something. I don't mean that he's condescending or patronizing—not a bit. But he's explaining farming—crops and livestock—to us as though we are from another planet. And it's fantastic! Maybe it's only really and truly striking to me as I'm the one person in the group who's ever lived on a farm. But it makes the whole experience so unexpectedly exotic.

We're so caught up in the tour that we nearly miss it. In our defence I don't think any of us were really thinking about how far east we'd travelled. Wainwright is a fair distance east of Edmonton, and then we'd travelled another couple of hours after that. Mr. Ford mentions that we're nearly at our destination. Then we see it. The sign.

We have just driven across the border to Saskatchewan! We are in SASKATCHEWAN!

Really, perhaps you don't understand the significance of this. This is cataclysmic, shattering, life altering. We are an ALBERTA road trip outfit. Our raison d'etre is investigating every nook and cranny of ALBERTA. Sometimes twice. We have vowed never to travel anywhere else (on the road trip). This weird twist of fate—the bison ranch straddling the Alberta–Saskatchewan border—may change the course of history. Thank goodness we weren't together in the same vehicle, or goodness knows what would have happened. (At the very least we would have driven off the road.) As we were separated from one another at this most crucial moment, I think you'll just have to imagine our BG spirits hovering over the highway, approximately one hour and a half east of Provost, Alberta. Just inside the Saskatchewan border.

Scene: The Gals Huddle Together Like A Bunch Of Helium Balloons

Me: I feel . . . funny.

Brian: Me too.

Tyler: (*belches*) Me too.

Me: Not like that, silly! I mean . . . metaphysically.

Brian: What's that smell? It's like baking bread, the forest after a rainfall, baby's breath . . .

Richard: It smells like . . . socialism.

Robert: You mean sort of, soft on crime . . . ?

Patti: (*dreamily*) There IS no crime here . . .

Brian: Um, I'm feeling all sort of . . . all gooey and . . . expansive toward my fellow citizens—

Me: (*horrified*) You?

Kevin: Whoa-whoa!

Me: (*always the first to be compassionate and caring*) What?

Kevin: I have vertigo! It feels like we're tilting!

Tyler: Yeah!

Brian: We're leaning to the left!!

Norma: Actually, after years of NDP, the reigning government here now is the centre right Saskatchewan Party, an amalgamation of Liberals and Conservatives.

Patti: (*still dreamily*) But it's not REALLY Conservative— it's not a soul-destroying, mean-spirited reign of terror, clear-cutting health, education, and social programs with an arrogant disregard for quality of

234

life. No, it's a sort of cozy, big-hearted, fair-minded, Saskatchewan version of being Conservative.

Norma: True.

Stephen: Unlike our BC Liberals who are more like Alberta Tories.

Norma: True.

Kevin: (*the voice of reason*) We still have to deal with the fact that we've ended up in Saskatchewan, folks.

Richard: Utopia . . .

Robert: (*excited*) What would happen if the Buffalo Gals started to go on trips here—in Saskatchewan?

Bob: What if we just moved here?

All: Maybe! I dunno! Hey, that's a great idea!

Me: (*babbling, incoherent*) So tired—so tired of barking for treats, they love writers in Saskatchewan, must be something in the water, isn't potash nicer than oil, cheaper real estate, even bigger sky, less traffic—

Robert: And rats!

(A moody silence descends on the group.)

Me: Oh look we're at the bison ranch.

The moody silence lifts once we realize that although we set foot into the province of Saskatchewan, our van did not. An excellent reprieve . . .

This may be the first time on any of our trips that the Buffalo Gals have wanted to adopt someone. And no I don't mean one of the fuzzy little bison calves. I mean Carl and Irma Rehman, who, along with their son Bob, own and operate the Border Bison Ranch in er, um . . . Macklin, Saskatchewan. Or maybe what we're really hoping is that they'll adopt us.

I don't think I ever really and truly understood the term "salt of the earth" until I met lanky, affable Bob, his clear-eyed, amazingly fit father, Carl—who's somewhere in his seventies but leaps about like a gazelle—and the divine Irma, a tiny, big-hearted dynamo who has spent half of her life raising umpteen children and the other half making pies.

The first stop on the tour involves retail-retail-retail. The Rehmans have refurbished a tiny little wooden garage right beside their house and filled it with buffalo goodies. There's all manner of bison paraphernalia, including gorgeous handmade gloves, but the real item is the buffalo rug on the wall. Norma positively levitates with joy; the ensuing bargaining process is brief and painless. (Norma makes an offer and Carl accepts.) Patti and Richard buy gloves—now we are more or less retail-sated. (At least till tomorrow.)

It's miserable out by now, blustery and rainy, but we're off to see the Rehmans's bison herd. Bob drives us right out into their midst;

Norma drives a bargain.
PHOTO: PATTI PON

safely ensconsed in his truck, we can peer out the window and marvel. Let me tell you, no one is offering to leap out of the vehicle and commune with the big bubbas, cause they are terrifyingly huge. And surly-looking. Though there are a few fuzzy little calves mixed in with the crowd to take the edge off the proceedings.

Bob regales us with tales depicting the sheer brute force of these animals. Then he guides us through their system of corrals and shutes, explaining every aspect of animal husbandry and patiently answering our dumb-ass questions. Still, I thought we were quite credible as an audience until I looked over and saw Tyler hopping from one foot to the other. I sidle up to him. "*What* are you doing?!" I whisper, all the while shooting anxious smiles at Bob Rehman. Tyler explains that he's jumping back and forth between Saskatchewan and Alberta.

Okay, he didn't actually do that. I'm lying. Though it does seem like the sort of thing Tyler might do. The sort of thing he *could* do actually, because the Saskatchewan–Alberta border runs right through the ranch. The Rehmans even have a monument marker in their yard, delineating the border between our two sweet prairie siblings.

Throughout this part of the tour we have an ongoing relationship with the Rehmans's dog Rex, who likes to sidle up, lean hard into your leg . . . and grunt. It's strange and endearing. Rex the Grunting Dog, for reasons known only to him, particularly loves Norma . . .

In the time-honoured tradition of the Buffalo Gals' clear-eyed culinary approach, we now prepare to eat some of the very animals we have just watched frolicking (okay, meandering) in a field. Only there's a problem, see, because usually Irma would lay out the food in their cavernous machine shed where we would eat at picnic tables. On this particular day, however, it is deemed to be just too darned cold. We stand around in the machine shed and visit for a while, drinking hot coffee. Irma makes a pronouncement. She can't stand the thought of us being vaguely uncomfortable whilst eating our dinner. Instead, she's going to rearrange the furniture in her tiny, tiny house so that we can all sit indoors.

Bob starts the bison steaks on the barbecue in the machine shed—yum—while Jennifer helps Irma reorganize her house to accommodate sixteen folks. (Us plus the Fords and the Rehmans.) Eight or nine of us will be seated at the kitchen table, with the rest seated in the living room, using little fold-out coffee trays as tables. Dinner—pardon me—"supper" is served buffet style. We pick up a plate and make our way along Irma's L-shaped counter, picking up bison steak, baked potatoes, and a selection of salads. All delicious. Bob, hailing from Montreal as he does, has never had ambrosia salad! Brian and I happily elaborate on all the different variations of this prairie culinary mainstay. (Please refer to Appendix Four for a recipe.) Immediately following dinner, as per prairie farm tradition, we have dessert. PIE-PIE-PIE! Banana cream, cherry, and the rare, seldom-sited, oft dreamed-of sour cream raisin pie. This is like finding a wild lady slipper or a four-leaf clover. (Please refer to Appendix Four for a recipe.) We are immediately pitched back to the Three Hills pie restaurant. I am hurled back to Ponoka, c. 1967 . . .

But the main event is the amazing Irma. She's a great storyteller, and she regales us with tales of flipping hundreds of bison burgers at the World Championship Bannock Games. (A sort of bone-throwing tournament.) Making pies to sell at a nearby farmer's market till she was pretty much rolling pastry in her dreams. Making gloves to sell to us.

These warm-hearted, charming, generous people work sooooo hard. And though I'm sure we all feel like Irma deserves time off in lieu for the rest of her life—in Hawaii—I'm not entirely sure she'd have it any other way. She is the picture of contentment.

Late that night we make our way back to Wainwright for a nightcap (= mojitos) at the Honey Pot Restaurant. Uneventful. We're too tired to have an event. The following morning we enjoy the final element of our package deal, breakfast at the Galleria restaurant, buy out the gift shop in the train station, and head out. (Patti buys commemorative buffalo pins for the three of us who have been on every trip. Nice!)

Sundays are difficult with this crew. Chances are, the most bally-hooed event of the weekend has already taken place, so there's a slightly anticlimactic feel to the proceedings. And by midafternoon, minds inevitably begin to turn to the week ahead. That said, there's a gentle buzz of anticipation about our planned Sunday afternoon activity.

The little hamlet of Paradise Valley is about fifty kilometres northeast of Wainwright. (There's some low-level anxiety about accidentally ending up in Saskatchewan, but we agree to keep a close watch on road signage and the map.) The inspiration for this little jaunt is the Climb Through Time Museum, displaying "fascinating artifacts and art portraying the birth of agriculture in Western Canada." (You know us—we're all about the artifacts and the agriculture.) The weather has finally turned mild and sunny as we pull into the deserted parking lot.

The design of the museum is truly unique. A slowly rising ramp spirals up through the centre of a grain elevator, with displays on either side of the path. It's lovely and quaint. Some of us end up in the tiny gift shop café toward the end of our visit. There's hilarity about something. Probably some inappropriately loud badinage. We're probably wearing our matching T-shirts. Finally, it proves to be too much for the volunteer on duty. "Excuse me, I don't mean to be rude, but who ARE you people?" I think Patti actually tries to explain . . .

Now it's time to do one of our dumb-ass, ill-conceived hurtles back toward home base. Remember the death-defying drive from High River to Calgary International Airport in year two? This ranks right up there. We absolutely had to stop at the beautiful Battle River Trestle Bridge just west of Wainwright. (That sets us back a bit, but it's totally worth it.) But then, after discovering that the Norwegian restaurant in Camrose is closed, and even though no one is actually hungry, and, additionally, WITHOUT actually calculating travel time back to Edmonton, we stop at a Boston Pizza restaurant for a meal and our final (financial) reckoning. Gee, guess what? The whole event took longer than twenty minutes.

Slow Boston Pizza
The outside world encroaches
We speed on Highway
—anonymous Gal

Now we have to drive like maniacs to get back to the city. Brian has a rehearsal, or auditions, or some bloody thing he has to attend. Tyler has to catch a plane. The last hour and a half of the trip is a bit of a nail-biter. The thought bubble above the van might read: "Monday. I totally forgot that Monday comes after Sunday . . ."

Airplanes, auditions
And the Red Arrow Express
Time to say goodbye

Still, notes from the scrapbook reflect some last-minute brainstorming about next year's trip.

1. Jasper: hot springs, whitewater rafting, needs a silly quotient, theme?

2. Cypress Hills: four days required?

3. Grande Prairie: definitely a fly-in

4. "The Rapture" tour featuring Rosebud Theatre, a reprise of the Passion Play and Creation Museum

5. Fort McMurray???

6. Someplace, anyplace where we might experience a Legion meat draw.

Most importantly, no one even questions the idea of going on, charging into a second decade of Buffalo Gals. I don't know about you, but I'm voting for "The Rapture . . ."

Wainwright Train Station.

PHOTO: JENNIFER FORD

TWENTY-THREE
BUFFALO GALS—
THE WAY AHEAD

How long will we keep going with this kooky initiative? Dunno.
Probably as long as we're able. There were actually a few jokes this
year about Buffalo Gal dementia. Or the wheelchair ramp into the
van. Maybe when we're old we really could drive around a parking lot
at a mall for thirty-six hours and have a high old time. This is a new
slant to our humour. I'm not sure I like it. Okay, it scares the hell out
of me.

But it's also kind of sweet: the assumption that we'll still be together
years from now. That come what may, we'll make the trip happen.

Come what may.

Our lives are happening to us, between Buffalo Gals road trips,
with or without our cooperation. Several of the Gals have lost a parent
or a sibling over the last nine years. There's some grey hair under the
Gopher Museum ball caps. We quietly register the life changes and
inevitable losses, knowing these sorrows will come to us all.

And lest I mire our little rowboat in sadness, let me say that many of the shifts and changes are, of course, ecstatically happy. We happily track the achievements and promising career moves in our group, and in our extended families and social circles.

It just seems like . . . at every stage of life you leave something behind in order to gain something else. (You're blissfully partnered to your new wife, so you see less of your dear friends; you start your own business, but you have to move to a new city.) That's life, we say. Or, priorities have changed. Or . . .

Maybe that's one of the reasons Buffalo Gals is so precious; it's a tradition we have been successful in maintaining throughout moves to other cities, career changes, births and deaths, and just the general chaos that usually leaves you feeling you're too busy to have fun.

We soldier on with our blind devotion to the concept. And we're rewarded with memories, mouth-watering meals, breath-taking hilarity, natural beauty, the cast of exceptional characters we meet on the road, and our own growing bond.

Someday . . . when we do end the tour, I still think we should leap off the edge of the cliff at Head-Smashed-In Buffalo Jump. And only after a crime spree through southern Alberta. Yipppeeee-kay-yay!!

Or maybe we'll just have one last night like our evening at Goldeye Centre. Hanging out around the fire, playing poker, dissecting and resolving the great cultural issues of our time, declaring ourselves well-pleased with dinner.

Buffalo Gals won't you come out tonight—and dance by the light of the moon . . .

APPENDIX ONE

THINGS YOU SHOULD TAKE ON YOUR ROAD TRIP

1. Snacks. Try to resist the temptation to buy cheddar cheese popcorn, it's really messy, especially for the driver.

2. Speaking of which, a coupla containers of "Wet Ones" would not go amiss.

3. Yer pals.

4. Craft bag: glue sticks, scissors, felt markers, scrapbook, reference books (*Norton Anthology of English Literature* or a recent *National Enquirer*).

5. Songbooks. Okay, honestly, this initiative has never met with much success on our trip, but I think you oughta give it a try.

6. A budget. Or, alternatively, a charge card with a sky-high limit.

7. An itinerary that you are passionate about but not married to.

8. A map, compass, or divining rod.

9. Clean underwear. Toothbrush. Deodorant. Honestly, you won't need anything else. Once you get your special T-shirt you'll just wear that all weekend anyway.

10. A digital camera, video camera, or voice recorder for recording the good bits. Or in case of litigation.

APPENDIX TWO

TEN THINGS THAT MAKE THE BUFFALO GALS SQUEAL
WITH DELIGHT
- Buffet
- Bacon
- Beef
- Souvenir shop
- Buffalo
- Martini bar
- Beef jerky
- World's largest anything
- Grade A anything
- Festival of anything

APPENDIX THREE

WEED WHACKERS

Butterball

Butter tart

Shutterbug

Buster crab

Pumper truck

Slumber party

Rocker world

Whistle-blower

Wrecker ball

Rockefeller

Lighter fluid

Springer spaniel

Gladiator

Washerwoman

Poker stick

Poker hand/face/game/table/chip

Upper case

Upper shelf

Upper Volta

Razor edge

Adjudicator

Germinator

Pumpernickel

Dictator

Oliver Twist

Fiddler on the Roof

Moby Dick upper level

Liquor board/barn/outlet/hutch/depot

Inner thigh

Inner Mongolia

Upper Sackville
Whippersnapper
Pincher Creek
Wicker basket
Inner tube
Inner sanctum
Inner ear
Cedar chest
Inspector Gadget
Smelter
Rectum
Dictum
Rubber dinghy
Rubbermaid
Rubber hose
Rubber glove
Rubber ducky
Rubber boot
Rubber sole

YOU CAN PLAY TOO—IT'S EASY AND FUN FOR THE
WHOLE FAMILY!

APPENDIX FOUR–RECIPES

AMBROSIA SALAD (one of many, many variations on this recipe)
   2 cans pineapple chunks, drained
   2 cans mandarin oranges, drained
   2 jars maraschino cherries, drained
   1 can coconut flakes
   ½ bag mini-marshmallows
   4 ounces sour cream
   16 ounces Cool Whip

   Combine sour cream and Cool Whip, stir in other ingredients. Chill for at least two hours before serving.

SOUR CREAM RAISIN PIE
   1 cup sugar
   ½ teaspoon cinnamon
   ½ teaspoon ground allspice
   ¼ teaspoon salt
   2 eggs beaten
   1 cup sour cream
   2 tablespoons vinegar
   1 cup raisins
   1 pie shell, unbaked, 9 inch

   In mixing bowl, combine sugar, spices, salt, and eggs; mix well. Blend in sour cream and vinegar; add raisins, stirring to blend. Pour into pie shell. Bake at 350 degrees for one hour or until set. Let pie cool at room temperature. Serve with ice cream or whipped cream, if desired.

ACKNOWLEDGMENTS

I am deeply appreciative of all the first-rate Alberta hospitality we've experienced over a decade of road trips. Heartfelt thanks to everyone we've encountered along the way—you were my inspiration. I also owe a huge debt of gratitude to all who guided and supported the process of writing and publishing this account of our adventures, including:

Linda Goyette (if not for you . . .), Gillian Steward, my fabulous editor, and all the marvellous folks at Brindle & Glass, a crack team led by the splendid Ruth Linka. Thanks to Gail Sobat (for YouthWrite and that first read), to Liz Grieve (for the seed of an idea), and to the Edmonton Arts Council for supporting this new direction. Finally, none of this would have been possible without the endless indulgence of beloved Bob Erkamp, Brian Deedrick, John Paul Fischbach, Stephen Heatley, James Tyler Irvine, Norma Lock, Kevin McGugan, Richard Stuart, and Bob White.

Conni Massing is an award-winning playwright and screenwriter whose work has been recognized by the Alberta Motion Picture Industries Association, the Academy of Cinema and Television, the Betty Mitchell Awards for theatre, and the Elizabeth Sterling Haynes Awards for theatre, and the Writers Guild of Alberta. A recipient of a Queen's Jubilee Medal, Conni was honoured as one of a hundred people who have made a contribution to Alberta theatre in the last one hundred years. She is the current writer-in-residence at the Edmonton Public Library and is a sessional instructor in playwriting and screenwriting at the University of Alberta. Born and raised in central Alberta, Conni lives in Edmonton.